Dish & Tell

Recipes from the Heart

SARAH PETERSON

Dish & Tell

Recipes from the Heart

SARAH PETERSON

MINNESOTA HISTORICAL SOCIETY PRESS

To Mom, for showing me what it means to cook and bake with love.

To Dad, for reminding me why we do it.

And to all the home cooks who are the keepers of their family's beloved recipes and food traditions.

For information, write to the Minnesota Historical Society Press, 345 Kellogg Blvd. W., St. Paul, MN 55102–1906.

mnhspress.org @mnhspress

The Minnesota Historical Society Press is a member of the Association of University Presses.

Manufactured in the United States of America.

10 9 8 7 6 5 4 3 2 1

∞ The paper used in this publication meets the minimum requirements of the American National Standard for Information Sciences—Permanence for Printed Library Materials, ANSI Z39.48–1984.

ISBN: 978-1-68134-329-7 (paperback)

Library of Congress Control Number: 2025943489

All recipes come from somewhere. Some family favorites may have first appeared on product packaging or in the pages of a decades-old community cookbook. Others were borrowed, shared, and handed down. Over time, we make them our own by tweaking a technique or adjusting an ingredient until the dish feels just right at our table. And then it becomes our version, ready to be passed along again.

Images on pages iv, 7, 8, 10, 12, 17, 25, 30, 56, 59, 60, 80, 87, 93, 106, 115, 128, 138, 152, 164, 168, 177, 215, 217, and 218: Rachael White at Set the Table Photography. Family photos courtesy recipe contributors. All others from the author's collection.

vi Preface

1 Introduction

5 The Keepers

9 The Heart of the House

13 Beloved Breakfasts

31 Morning Sweets & Coffee Treats

61 Memorable Mains & Sides

89 Sentimental Soups & Grandma Bread

107 Potlucks & Party Food

129 Sweet Memories

177 Treasured Holiday Traditions

212 Index

216 Photo Captions

217 Weights & Measures

218 Acknowledgments

preface

When I put pen to paper to write this book, I never expected it would parallel one of the most challenging times for my family. However, it was a period that, again and again, reinforced the meaning behind recipes from the heart.

My dad's pancreatic cancer diagnosis in 2021 put our family in a tailspin as we navigated a new world of ongoing scans, chemo, radiation, and endless doctor appointments. The proverbial table had turned, and I had to "be there" for my parents in northern Minnesota to help and support them through this difficult role reversal as I became a caregiver to the ones who had always cared for me. Beyond driving them to appointments and various other tasks, I felt compelled to nurture my parents. And one of the only ways I knew how to do this was through food.

Whether it was bringing my dad a special treat like his favorite cinnamon rolls from Tobie's in Hinckley (a convenient halfway point between my home and my parents' house) or hotdish to stock their freezer, I never showed up empty-handed. When we were together, we'd dine at our favorite Duluth restaurants as we went to and from doctor's appointments. I'd bake my dad's favorite goodies alongside my mom in the cozy kitchen of my childhood home. We'd enjoy home-cooked meals—just the three of us—around their dining room table.

As awful as it is to witness a parent go through an extended illness, this period gave me the unexpected gift of *time* with my mom and dad. We had the opportunity to enjoy many, many meals and treats together and bond over our favorite family recipes. And for that, I will be forever grateful.

When my dad learned I was writing this book, he kept a food diary to chronicle every meal my mom made for him on a daily basis. The list included many of the familiar meals we had when I was growing up, like spaghetti and garlic bread or Sunday dinner with pork *and* roast beef, along with simpler items such as crescent wieners, tuna salad (yes, the kind with shoestring potatoes), or Spam sandwiches. My mom was always ready to prepare something that appealed to my dad, and after more than fifty years of marriage she knew his palate better than anyone.

My dad sent me frequent emails with pictures he took with his iPad to capture my mom's baking, from her famous chocolate cake to her signature decorated sugar cookies. He was always so grateful and proud. During the thick of the COVID-19 pandemic and being stuck at home, he wrote, "IF you are going to be stranded with someone, your MOTHER is the one. She has such a wealth of knowledge when it comes to baking and cooking almost anything. EVERY DAY brings something new and delicious! I GUESS I'M VERY, VERY LUCKY!!! 💗💕💗 Dad."

To me, the meals my mom lovingly prepared for my dad, as well as the endless sweets, are a true testament to cooking from the heart. Whether it's a humble everyday meal or a special treat, food is a powerful expression of love, comfort, and connection. Cherished family recipes do more than nourish our bodies—they lift our spirits, bring us together, and leave lasting imprints on our hearts.

introduction

I believe the very best, most memorable meals are those made with love in the kitchens of our families and friends.

Sure, there are noteworthy restaurant meals that have knocked my socks off and stand out for their impeccable presentation, their use of fine ingredients, or the ambiance of the dining establishment. Still, if you ask me what I would like for my last meal, I would happily forgo dinner at a fancy-schmancy restaurant and emphatically tell you I would like to have my mom's Italian shells, served with her pillowy soft garlic bread followed by a very large serving of the decadent chocolate cake she has made every year for my birthday since I was a young girl. And the entire meal would be served on my grandma's vintage Homer Laughlin china with the sweet floral pattern, thank you very much.

The recipes passed down in my family—like Grandma Hilma's rusks, Aunt Ede's meatballs, and my mom's chocolate chip shortbread cookies—are the ones I turn to over and over again when I cook for my own family and friends and will always have a home in my recipe box.

Every family has certain dishes they hold dear to their heart: It could be a beloved dish that shows up on the regular at family celebrations, holidays, or other special occasions. Perhaps it's a dish tied to a childhood memory or a loved one. If you are lucky, you may have your family recipes recorded and preserved in a special cookbook. Or maybe you have a recipe box that belonged to your mom or grandma that's complete with your family's handwritten heirloom recipes. Perhaps YOU are the special force whose own recipes bring joy to the tables of your friends and family. Regardless of where your recipes are physically housed, the memories tied to these special dishes are powerful connections to the past and an important part of every family's history and legacy.

I've spent the past few years gathering and preserving my family's most cherished recipes, along with the stories of the incredible women who made them. In this book you'll find those recipes, as well as contributions from others in our great state who've generously shared their own family favorites. Through a foodie version of "show and tell" that I call "dish and tell," I've had the privilege of hearing stories about the recipes that people hold close to their hearts, the traditions that keep them alive, and the loved ones who made them special. I've learned that people love "dishing" about their family's special recipes and that there is a healthy appetite for tried-and-true recipes from other passionate home cooks.

This book is a celebration of those recipes with heart—the dishes that nourish our bodies, fill our souls, and connect us across generations. I hope these stories inspire you to try some new-to-you recipes, reminisce about the meals that shaped you, and perhaps even "dish and tell" with your own loved ones, ensuring your treasured recipes and family's food traditions live on.

XOXO,
Sarah

Recipes from the Heart: Defined

1. Home-cooked meals or morsels that are a gesture of love and care, a symbol of celebration, a welcome blast from the past—evoking memories of a special loved one or a significant place and time.

2. The distinctive cuisine from the epicenter of America's heartland: Minnesota! With Native American roots, an abundance of local agriculture, and a rich culture of immigrants, our great state is a smorgasbord of familiar favorites and diverse flavors and a reflection of those who live here: warm, welcoming, and full of tradition.

Recipes from the heart are:

Communal Many of us have special traditions centered around the making of a family recipe together with several loved ones taking part. In my family, this is lefse. Leading up to the holidays, we gather to mash and prep the potatoes, roll the dough, carefully maneuver the lefse to and from the hot griddle, and, finally, sample the results of our hard work.

For others I talked to, the dishes they make as a family include everything from Easter pies and potica to pasties and poppy kuchen. It's true that "many hands make light work," but more often than not this shared time is about the camaraderie of being together, keeping up traditions, passing down knowledge, and making new memories.

Community-focused When large groups come together for a meal such as a potluck, recipes from the heart take center stage. We bring forth the best of the best from our home kitchens that we feel are worthy to share and that we know are tried-and-true, people-pleaser menu items to feed a crowd, whether it's a large pasta salad, a scrumptious dip, or a pan of bars. Church and community cookbooks, lovingly compiled by members of a congregation or specific group, are full of these recipes. The collaborative efforts are often used as fundraisers, reinforcing the idea of community and working toward a common goal.

Celebratory Food and celebration go hand in hand. Life's milestone moments—birthdays, graduations, baby showers—all call for special celebratory foods, and the festive recipes served often hold deep sentimental value. A birthday cake baked with love, a gorgeously decorated sandwich loaf, or the treasured treats and traditional dishes reserved for the holidays—these moments become even more special when tied to a dish that has been passed down through generations.

Comforting There are certain dishes we turn to in times of stress or sadness or simply when we need to feel at home. Whether it's mom's meatloaf, a cozy breakfast like a Dutch pancake, or the smell of cinnamon rolls baking in the oven, these recipes go beyond satisfying hunger to wrap us in a comforting blanket of warmth and nostalgia.

Caring From preparing a care package for a friend who needs a lift to baking cookies to brighten someone's day to making a loved one's favorite meal, food is a universal way to show we care. Nourishing chicken soup, a comforting casserole or hotdish, a loaf of fresh banana bread—these are examples of the recipes we associate with caretaking, and sharing them reminds someone they are loved.

Connective Recipes can be a link to our past, to the people we hold dear, and to the cultures that shaped us. Many families have dishes that have been handed down through the generations—recipes that connect them to their ancestors or a beloved family member. Perhaps it's a cherished bread recipe from a grandmother, homemade noodles that remind someone of a childhood spent in their parents' kitchen, or an heirloom recipe prepared each holiday. There is a sense of pride that comes with sharing a piece of our history or culture and carrying on treasured family traditions to the next generation.

Dish & Tell: Preserving Your Family's Food Traditions

A cherished family recipe, while undoubtedly delicious, represents so much more than food. It's a story, a tradition, a way to connect. When we "dish and tell," we not only share the special recipes that have shaped our lives and the stories that make those dishes unforgettable, we preserve memories and important traditions. If you are lucky, you have this treasured history handwritten on cards and tucked into the time capsules we call recipe boxes or family cookbooks. But many of us have felt the sadness of realizing that no one wrote down Grandma's traditional cookie recipe or that we never thought to ask a beloved aunt for her signature dish.

I think often about my grandmothers and special aunts who were long gone by the time I developed an interest in cooking and baking. I have wonderful memories of time spent around their tables, enjoying their homemade dishes. But what I wouldn't give to go back in time, to chitchat in their kitchens, to pick their brains about the recipes and the techniques they perfected over decades. I would ask Grandma Hilma about her perfect buns that no one seems to have a recipe for. I'd ask Aunt Ede about her tricks for making melt-in-your-mouth divinity, and I'd ask Grandma Frances for her Black Forest cake recipe.

The realization of how much I wish I had learned from them has fueled my passion for preserving family food traditions today. I am incredibly grateful to have my mom, Carol, and my mother-in-law, Mary Lou, to turn to for family recipes. They not only share handwritten recipes from yesteryear and lend me their well-used cookbooks, but they also spend time baking and cooking with me. These moments are a true gift, a treasure I will forever cherish.

As I've been interviewing others for my blog and this book, I've loved hearing how they are reaching out and connecting with family members who are the keepers of cherished recipes. I've witnessed firsthand the joy and pride these families feel when given the opportunity to revisit old recipes, reminisce, and share their stories.

My greatest hope is that this book inspires you to cook and bake with your loved ones, share your own family's special recipes, preserve traditions, and make new memories in the process.

Tips to Dish & Tell

Stir Up Memories

If you want to preserve your family's food traditions, start by asking elder family members or loved ones about their favorite foods and food memories. Look through their recipe boxes, cookbooks, and photo albums. Here are a few conversation starters:

- What is a favorite dish from your childhood or a dish that reminds you of home?
- Are there special foods your family had at the holidays or for celebrations?
- If you could pass down one family recipe, what would it be? Who used to make it?

Get Cooking

If you have a favorite dish someone in your family makes, ask to make it alongside them. Involve others in the family and make a fun day of it. Or make the act of "dish and telling" a gift—for them and you!

Package a wooden spoon, a pretty bowl, or a baking dish along with some ingredients and an invitation to "dish and tell." When the day arrives, make them feel like the guest of honor—gather all the ingredients, help with prep, and handle the cleanup. Encourage them to bring out their recipe box, old cookbooks, and family photo albums. Ask about the foods they grew up with, their fondest kitchen memories, and their favorite family recipes. Don't forget to document the day: Take pictures, record a video, or write down the stories shared.

Start a Dish & Tell Club (Recipe Card Swap)

Pick a theme (e.g., weeknight dinners, family favorites, party appetizers, sweets/desserts). Invite friends and family to join and ask everyone to write their favorite recipe on recipe cards. The number of recipe cards should equal the number of people in the recipe card swap.

When it comes to distributing the recipes, you could:

- Host an in-person event with all participants. Each participant brings their set of recipe cards. Place the stacks of cards around a table and have everyone walk around to collect one recipe from each pile to make their own collection to take home for their personal recipe box. You might also invite everyone to make their recipe to bring to the event to share.
- Share a list with everyone's mailing address. Each participant mails their recipe to everyone on the list. If you have ten people in your "club," they each send out nine recipes—and then they get nine in return.
- In this digital world, you could have participants type their recipes and conduct the swap via email, but consider offering a fun digital recipe card template that everyone can use for consistency and to create a nice keepsake.

Host a Dish & Tell Party

Similar to a cookbook club, open up your home to host a potluck-style party where you invite family and friends to share a handed-down dish along with the recipe. Suggest a theme or meal (like breakfast or dinner), and have guests sign up for different components of the menu (appetizers, salads, entrees, desserts). As guests sample the offerings, encourage them to "dish and tell," sharing the stories behind their recipes.

For the Keepers—Those Who Hold Family Recipes

- Invite your family members to your kitchen to cook together.
- If you use a specific dish or if certain cooking utensils or tools are needed for a favorite family recipe, give the item as a gift along with your recipe.
- Share a recipe box with your handwritten recipes or make a recipe book to give as a gift for graduation, a housewarming, a wedding, etc. You will see several examples of family cookbooks throughout this book, from photocopied pages with handwritten recipes to spiral-bound, published books.

the keepers

Most of the recipes I hold dear to my heart are connected to the special women in my life: my grandmothers, my great-aunt Ede, my mom, and my mother-in-law, as well as my husband's grandmothers. Some of their cherished recipes live on recipe cards, handwritten by the very person who first shared them at a meal or gathering. Others have been duplicated, rewritten, and passed down through multiple generations but will be forever tied to that one particular person whose signature dish has brought so much joy to the table over the years.

I consider myself—or anyone else in possession of family recipes that they continue to make and share—to be a "keeper": the caretaker of those beloved dishes that represent their family's history, culture, and traditions. They hold the key to the past and are most often the ones who possess the family recipes (whether written down or in their head), continue to make their family's favorite dishes for holidays and special occasions, and play a role in passing on their family's recipes and important traditions to the next generation.

There are many keepers in my family whom I've loved tapping through the past few years to collect and share our most cherished recipes. But at the core are the following ladies, the ones I consider to be the original keepers for their role in shaping the food traditions that my family still celebrates today and whose recipes and stories you'll see referenced throughout the book.

Carol

My mom, Carol, grew up in Bemidji, Minnesota, before meeting my dad in college and eventually settling in Cloquet, Minnesota, where they lived in the same house for more than fifty years. Her love of antiques and vintage dishes spilled into every room of the house, but her true passion was always in the kitchen.

A devoted mother and homemaker, she embodies cooking from the heart, from her robust holiday baking to her Sunday dinners and everything in between. When I think of the countless hours she has logged in the kitchen, all I can say is uff da! But she never complained. For her, caring for our family through food was her labor of love.

Her food is always delicious, never a dud in her rotating menu of family favorites that includes Italian shells, Sunday roast with perfect gravy, chocolate chip shortbread cookies, chocolate-covered cherry bars, chocolate cake, and so many other fabulous recipes.

Hilma

My mom's mother, Hilma, whom we called Grandma Meland, was the ultimate grandmother. From her perfectly set hair that had a purplish undertone to her distinctive scent that was a mixture of freshly baked cookies and Jean Naté, my grandma was so much fun to visit at her home in Bemidji, Minnesota.

One summer, when I was around twelve years old, I took a three-hour Greyhound bus ride from Cloquet to spend an entire week with her. We spent the days watching game shows and soap operas (which I loved), and my grandma would make us a home-cooked meal at lunch and dinner—always served with some type of dessert.

Like many women in her generation, my sweet grandma was happiest when she was feeding others. With Norwegian roots, she loved her lefse and lutefisk, but some of my family's favorite dishes from Hilma included her delicious rusks, homemade buns, beautiful blueberry pies, and an abundance of cookies tucked away in coffee tins in the deep freezer on the back porch.

Frances

Frances, my "Grandma Granley," was a career woman who worked as a secretary at the oil refinery in Carlton, Minnesota. Perhaps this role explains her appreciation for dining out over cooking. We had a special bond, and beginning when I was just a little girl, she'd pick me up on Saturday mornings for a full day of shopping and lunch at a nice restaurant in Duluth, where she'd always enjoy at least one Manhattan cocktail. Our "ladies' lunches" remained one of our favorite pastimes well into my adulthood.

When she did spend time in the kitchen, Grandma Granley had a flair for fancy desserts. On Sunday afternoons, my parents, brothers, and I would visit her and my grandpa to catch up on life, watch sports, and enjoy her special treats such as chocolate cherry cake or her strawberry or pineapple frozen desserts. She also was known for the delicious ham she'd serve for holidays, complete with raisin sauce and a side of her famous cheesy potatoes that she topped with sour cream and onion–flavored potato chips.

Ede

When my great-aunt Ede married, her new mother-in-law feared her son would starve due to Ede's lack of cooking skills. Little did she know, Ede would become the Martha Stewart of her time! A talented cook, baker, and gardener, she was also a masterful hostess who loved to entertain in her welcoming home, always with a perfectly set table. After retiring as a schoolteacher, she pursued quilting, another of her many talents.

In addition to the special tropical slush she'd keep on hand for drop-by guests, her signature dishes such as "Ede's meatballs," creamy cucumbers, and church egg dish all remain family favorites.

Mary Lou

I hit the jackpot when I married Jaye and gained my mother-in-law, Mary Lou. Raised on a farm near Roseau, Minnesota, she was tapped to cook and bake for her family at an early age. She also had a stint as a "church lady," serving as chair of the cookbook committee for a few years, which explains why I am the proud owner of several editions of *St. Philip the Deacon's Favorites* that happen to include recipes submitted by nearly everyone in our family, including my husband, Jaye.

In addition to being a bona fide lefse lady, Mary Lou is an all-around amazing cook who can whip up a meal on short notice with whatever ingredients she has on hand—no doubt the result of learning to be resourceful in her farm upbringing. She also makes holidays extra special and has an ease to entertaining, making everyone feel like a welcome guest. Besides lefse, Mary Lou's Hall of Fame foods include flatbread, krumkake, and Swedish meatballs.

Myrtle aka Gam

A proud German with a twinkle in her eye, my grandma-in-law Gam was an absolute joy to be around. I feel lucky to have had a seat at her table, where there was always so much laughter. She introduced me to many great dishes like ring-mac salad, German potato salad, ham loaf with mustard sauce, and hands down the best sloppy joes (made with a can of chicken gumbo soup, of course). Like my Grandma Granley, Gam worked outside of the home yet still found time to make delicious home-cooked meals for her family each night as well as do her fair share of entertaining. I cherish the cookbooks and recipes she left behind, especially her handwritten notes and menus from the holidays.

Charlotte

I never had the chance to meet my husband's grandmother Charlotte (Mary Lou's mom), but I feel I've come to know her through her many recipes we love today. She raised her family on a busy farm and spent a lot of time in her farmhouse kitchen with many mouths to feed several times a day—including two lunches at 9 a.m. and 3 p.m., with dinner served in between at noon.

It's been a treat to look through her old cookbooks and uncover some of her recipes in the notes section. Charlotte's easy yet delicious homemade pancakes, baked French toast, and never-fail donuts are staples in our family—not to mention her holiday must-haves like lefse and flatbread.

THE KITCHEN
The kitchen of the home is sacred ground,
Where loving and caring and sharing abound,
Where plans are made for the day ahead,
And where all gather for daily bread.
The kitchen provides food for the head and the heart,
And the energy for the day's fresh start.
Though in other parts of the house we may roam,
We return to the kitchen, the heart of the home.
—Allan G. Peterson

the heart of the house

The kitchen, where recipes from the heart come to life, is the heart of the house.

Beyond a place where we prepare meals day in and day out, our kitchens serve as command central for busy families, they are the place where everyone seems to congregate during parties, and they are the backdrop for countless shared moments. They hold memories of time spent connecting with loved ones, cooking and baking alongside one another or simply enjoying meals together.

Some of my earliest memories are in my grandmothers' kitchens, which were full of life and an abundance of sweet treats, laughter, and love.

My Grandma Hilma's kitchen was a hub of constant activity, particularly before family dinners. She didn't have a dining room, so the eat-in kitchen would transform from a flurry of meal prep—with my grandma and her sister Edna scurrying about—to a sit-down dinner at an impeccably set table that had been expanded to seat about a dozen cousins, aunts, uncles, and so on. My grandma had beautiful dishes—I don't remember ever using paper plates—including her everyday Homer Laughlin china as well as many heirloom serving bowls and platters, all easily accessible from the corner china closet right in the kitchen.

My Grandpa and Grandma Granley's kitchen was where we'd gather each Sunday afternoon for dessert, where my playful grandma would let me blow big soapy bubbles all over the table, and where I would bake the tiniest of cakes using my Betty Crocker oven. There was a set of swinging doors that masked the entry to the adjacent laundry room but made for some fun entertainment as my brothers and I loved to bust through them like a scene in an old Western movie.

Then there is my parents' kitchen, which served as the center point for nearly every milestone moment of my life for more than fifty years. It's where I first baked, using my *Better Homes and Gardens Junior Cookbook* to make snickerdoodles. It's where I watched my mom make countless meals and where I would bake alongside her, both as a young child and as an adult—and later with my kids joining us to make many of our family's cherished recipes. To some it may have appeared that "Carol's Kitchen" was stuck in an eighties time warp with its linoleum floors and the matching fruit-themed tile and stunning stained glass light fixture, but to me it was perfect in every way.

It probably comes as no surprise that these days my own kitchen is my happy place. It's where I retreat when I need to destress by baking or taking my time to make a leisurely home-cooked meal. It's where my family gathers when we are all home. It's the place where friends and family enter our home through the back door. (Only strangers or salespeople come to our front door.)

We have an older house (circa 1900), so our kitchen has evolved over the years. When we moved in, it had been moved from its original location to the back porch of the house. It was a galley or "one-butt kitchen" that served us well for more than ten years, but I was over the moon when we were able to expand it and add space for an eat-in area and more room to groove for preparing meals, entertaining, and the occasional dance party.

No matter the size or era of your kitchen, it needs to be functional above anything else. But we spend so much time in the kitchen that it should also be a comfortable and inviting space. For me this means adding some personal touches to pay tribute to the ladies in my life who have inspired me in the kitchen as well as to reflect my love of vintage dishes and my collection of recipe boxes. I also like to follow in the footsteps of culinary icon Julia Child, using cookware and utensils for decoration *and* function.

By surrounding yourself with items that tell your family's story, honor the cooks who came before you, or spark sweet memories, you turn your kitchen into more than a work-space: It becomes a place where your heart feels at home.

Tips to Show Your Heart in Your Kitchen

- Hang a cherished dish. Whether it's a single plate or a collage of vintage china, display family dishes that carry meaning and history.
- Frame and hang a beloved recipe. Preserve a handwritten recipe from a loved one and hang it where it can inspire your cooking and spark conversation.
- Display family photos, maybe of those who first taught you to cook or other favorites from your childhood.
- Create a cookbook nook to house family cookbooks or special ones from your childhood.
- Honor aprons of the past by installing a hook to hang aprons worn by loved ones, keeping their presence alive.
- Set up a memory corner with heirloom items (e.g., a set of mixing bowls, a rolling pin) that have been passed down to you, creating a cozy tribute spot.
- Make a playlist that connects you with the era of the person tied to a special recipe, bringing the past to life while you cook.

About the Recipes in This Book

The family-favorite dishes featured throughout this book were shared by real-life and "relatable" people—fellow passionate home cooks. While these recipes were not tested in a professional kitchen, you can take comfort in knowing that they have been made over and over again by their contributors and perfected through time.

Midwest Pantry Powerhouse Ingredients

In writing this cookbook, it was fun to get a glimpse into people's kitchens and pantries. One thing I learned is that savvy family cooks know when to take shortcuts by using a cake mix or refrigerated pie crust or when to use a can of condensed soup to add some flavor to a particular dish. And while outsiders may not always understand Minnesotans' passion for tater tots, Spam, or Top the Tater, I say let's proudly celebrate these Midwest delicacies for what they are and what they bring to the table.

For the most part the recipes in this book feature ingredients you can find at any major grocery retailer. There are a few instances, such as cracked wheat for tender "grandma bread" or bulk poppy seeds for poppy kuchen, that may require a little online sleuthing (Amazon) or a visit to an ethnic grocery store.

Following is a list of some of the powerhouse pantry items that passionate home cooks in Minnesota often keep in stock, including a number of underrated and underappreciated products.

Jell-O: Not just for stunning gelatin molds (although that is reason enough to stock an ample supply), Jell-O is handy to have on hand for a variety of desserts or to use as a thickening agent for certain recipes like rhubarb slush.

Instant pudding: A common ingredient in many vintage cakes and desserts, instant pudding helps improve the flavor and texture. It can also be used for old-fashioned frosting when mixed with Cool Whip and milk.

Boxed cake mixes: A handy help when you need a foolproof foundation for several great desserts from rum cake to self-filled cupcakes.

Spam: Delicious as an ingredient in some salads and main dishes, better when fried in a pan and served on buttered toast, and ingenious when the packaging is used as a cookie cutter for rectangular Aunt Sally cookies (see page 149).

Top the Tater: With the built-in flavors of onions and chives, this iconic dip can be used to make salad dressing or for any savory recipe that calls for sour cream, such as cheesy potatoes (page 191), creamy cucumbers (page 86), or dill pickle pasta salad (page 124).

Mini marshmallows: Often added to several different potluck salads, mini marshmallows (especially the colored ones) contribute flair and fun.

Maraschino cherries: Used as a colorful and retro garnish or the star ingredient in baked goods like cherry bread, chocolate-covered cherry bars, and more.

Condensed soups: Great for added flavor in a variety of hotdishes, meatballs, or slow cooker meals.

Other staples you will find in many Minnesota kitchens, including my own: tater tots, frozen walleye fillets, wild rice, and butter. So much butter!

Pillsbury
Better Homes and Gardens New Cook Book
The General Foods Kitchens COOKBOOK
Random House
The Joy of Cooking
Rombauer
Bobbs Merrill
French Cooking

Beloved Breakfasts

Here's what's cookin'

Frothy Orange Juice 15
Church Egg Dish 16
Akoori / Parsi Scrambled Eggs 18
Sour Milk Griddle Cakes 21
Baked French Toast 23
Dutch Pancake 24
Danish Puff 27

One of my favorite breakfast memories involves waking up at my grandparents' house after a weekend sleepover. Usually I'd stayed up late watching *The Love Boat* or *Donny & Marie*, and in the morning I'd wander downstairs to find Grandma Frances in her velour bathrobe, blending frothy orange juice. She'd pour it into a tall glass and let me choose a swizzle stick from her vast collection. It felt like such a treat—like she was making something special just for me.

Of course, there were pancakes and bacon or some other main course, but it's the orange juice that stands out in my mind because my grandma was making a fuss over me.

Other memorable breakfasts often revolved around the holidays, such as Easter brunch or Christmas morning, when there'd be a scrumptious egg bake, a beautiful fruit salad, and some type of sweet baked good. But there were also the not-too-fussy morning meals enjoyed with friends and family that were just as dear. I remember crowding into Grandma Hilma's friend Adele's tiny house, where she'd fittingly serve miniature silver dollar pancakes. We'd squeeze around her table to enjoy an endless supply of her fun-size pancakes.

Then there were the St. Paddy's Day potluck brunches my husband and I hosted in our early years as a young couple to "lay the base" for a day of festive shenanigans. It was fun to see the assortment of different egg bakes that would come through our door—and are probably the reason I have a surplus of left-behind glass casserole dishes to this day.

What I have learned is this: Breakfast is a blast with an abundance of friends and family, but there is also something special about simple dishes shared with our loved ones that makes them just as satisfying as any elaborate spread. I love learning about others' breakfast traditions, whether brunching with family and friends, special morning meals during the holidays, or more informal affairs on lazy weekends.

Frothy Orange Juice

the dish

The creamiest, smoothest orange juice, made effortlessly in a blender from frozen concentrate.

the tell

Before Orange Julius was even on my radar, I was crazy for creamy, blended orange juice thanks to my grandma Frances. She didn't need any fancy ingredients: She simply plopped frozen orange juice concentrate into a blender with some water. A few quick whirls and the result was a smooth, frothy texture that made plain old orange juice seem like a special treat.

Frozen orange juice concentrate may not be as commonly used today, but my grandma knew a good value when she saw it. There is also a convenience factor, as it can be tucked away in the freezer until needed. In my grandma's case, that was whenever the grandkids visited for a sleepover.

Sometimes we'd use the leftover juice to make mini OJ popsicles. We'd pour the juice into an ice cube tray, add a splash of 7UP, cover it with plastic wrap, and poke toothpicks through. A few hours in the freezer, and we had tiny, fizzy, citrusy treats—simple yet special, just like the frothy orange juice itself.

SERVES 6

1 (16-ounce) can frozen orange juice concentrate

Empty can of concentrate into a blender. Add 2 cans of water. Blend to desired state of frothiness. Serve immediately.

Church Egg Dish

the dish

A make-ahead breakfast casserole that's best when refrigerated overnight to be baked to its glorious, golden-brown state when you want to wake up to a no-fuss, amazing morning meal.

the tell

I credit many of my go-to recipes to my aunt Ede, but her church egg dish tops the list of dishes that grace our family's morning table several times throughout the year. We all love this tasty casserole, both for its ease of preparation and for how it includes all the components of a hearty and comforting breakfast—sausage, eggs, bread, and cheese—in one dish.

Ede was known for her seemingly effortless manner of serving amazing meals made from a short list of simple ingredients. While she often cooked and baked with the produce from her garden, she also looked to standard pantry ingredients and wasn't afraid to use a can of condensed soup or other canned goods when the occasion called for it. Her church egg dish reflects Ede's smart and simplified approach, using staple ingredients and prepping in advance. This dish is also best when made the day before for an added level of convenience any home cook will appreciate.

Judging by its name, I am sure church egg dish was one of Ede's many delicious contributions to the potluck-style breakfasts following church service in the fifties and sixties. It's the type of flavorful comfort food she was known for, and a crowd-pleasing dish that is meant to be shared at church and beyond.

SERVES 8–10

8 slices bread, cut into cubes

8 ounces shredded cheddar cheese

1 pound breakfast sausage links, browned and sliced

4 eggs

2¼ cups milk

½ teaspoon salt

¼ teaspoon pepper

pinch nutmeg, optional

Lightly grease a 9x13–inch casserole dish and add cubed bread. Layer cheese and sausage on top.

Mix eggs, milk, salt, pepper, and nutmeg (if using) in a bowl; pour over bread/sausage/cheese mixture. Cover and refrigerate overnight.

When ready to bake, heat oven to 325 degrees. Uncover and bake for about 45 minutes, until golden brown and bubbly.

tips Any kind of breakfast sausage will work. I prefer sausage links, often opting for the maple-flavored variety.

To make this dish gluten-free, use gluten-free bread or gluten-free stuffing mix (just the bread cubes; save the seasoning packet for another time).

Akoori / Parsi Scrambled Eggs

Louella Anderson
Eden Prairie, MN

the dish

Parsi scrambled eggs include a flavorful base of onions, turmeric, garlic, ginger, serrano chiles, tomatoes, and cilantro.

the tell

Louella, whose mom, Dolly, is Parsi, grew up with a front-row seat to a distinct style of cooking featuring a blend of hot and sweet flavors.

The Parsi people, who settled in Mumbai, India, from Iran in pursuit of religious freedom more than 1,200 years ago, developed a unique culture with cuisine that drew on the foods and ingredients in western India yet retained the flavors and techniques of ancient Persia. Staple ingredients in many Parsi dishes include onions, garlic, ginger, tomatoes, and chiles as well as spices such as turmeric, cumin, coriander, and chile powders.

While many Parsi dishes center around lentils or rice, eggs often play a starring role in dishes like akoori. Louella's mother would prepare this recipe on Sundays after church for a warm and satisfying family brunch. Hearty and shareable, akoori was the perfect dish for a household that included Louella, her parents, and three siblings.

Some of Louella's fondest food memories include her mother's kolmi no patio—succulent shrimp simmered in a rich tomato gravy, reminiscent of akoori's base, served over white rice. Another favorite was dhansak, a comforting dal slow-cooked with chicken or lamb and vegetables like eggplant, pumpkin, or squash, paired with caramelized rice and a refreshing side of cucumber, onion, and cilantro tossed in lime juice.

Today, Louella continues her mother's tradition, making akoori for herself and her husband, serving it alongside buttered toast, just as her mom did. "Akoori will always have a special place in my heart. The smell of the vegetables and spices cooking immediately brings me back to those Sunday mornings enjoying brunch with my family," says Louella. "Plus, it's quick and easy to prepare with ingredients many home cooks are likely to have on hand. It could easily work for a quick weeknight supper or as a weekend brunch."

tips **The recipe calls for ginger garlic paste that's sold in jars and can be found at Indian grocery stores, but an alternative is to substitute ½ teaspoon minced garlic and ½ teaspoon minced ginger.**

Pay attention to the color and texture of the sauce when simmering down the tomatoes. It should be a deep red color.

just for fun

When each of Louella's boys got married, she put together a recipe book for them with their favorite childhood recipes, some that she'd made (even if they didn't like them) and some from both sides of the family.

The oldest thing in Louella's kitchen is a solid brass mortar and pestle that belonged to her mom's great-aunt. It came from Persia and was used by her mom for years before she passed it on to Louella.

SERVES 4

2 tablespoons ghee or olive oil

2 small onions, sliced thin

3 green onions, both white and green parts, chopped

½ teaspoon ground turmeric

1 teaspoon ginger garlic paste (see tip)

2 serrano chiles, chopped (remove seeds for less heat)

½ cup chopped cilantro, divided

2 plum tomatoes, finely chopped

6 eggs, beaten

salt and pepper

for serving: buttered toast

Heat oil in a skillet over medium heat and cook onions until translucent. Add green onions and cook, stirring, for about a minute. Stir in turmeric and ginger garlic paste and continue cooking until onions start to brown. Add chiles and ¼ cup cilantro to the pan and cook 2–3 minutes over medium heat. Add tomatoes and stir well; continue cooking until tomatoes break up and liquid is boiled off. The mixture should be a dark red color. Stir in eggs and scramble to preferred consistency, watching so that they do not become too dry. Season with salt and pepper, and sprinkle with remaining cilantro. Serve with buttered toast.

Sour Milk Griddle Cakes

3 c. flour
1 tsp. soda
1 tsp. salt
1 tsp. melted fat.

1 tbsp. sugar
2½ c. s. milk or butter-milk
1 egg well-beaten

the dish

Fluffy and foolproof, these buttermilk pancakes made from a hundred-year-old recipe stand the test of time.

Sour Milk Griddle Cakes

the tell

My mother-in-law, Mary Lou, has always made the best, fluffiest pancakes. Her secret? A time-honored recipe passed down by her mother, Charlotte, from their days living on a farm near Roseau, Minnesota. The original recipe, called "Sour Milk Griddle Cakes," is written in one of Charlotte's old recipe books where there are several recipes that call for "sweet milk" while others, like these pancakes, list "sour milk" as an ingredient. Mary Lou explained that sweet milk meant regular drinking milk. For sour milk, her mom would add vinegar to sweet milk to make it sour since buttermilk wasn't readily available back then.

Mary Lou remembers her mother making these pancakes regularly—often in the size of a silver dollar, never too big but always in a plentiful supply.

"We didn't shop for groceries," she recalls. "We picked, canned, and froze garden fruit and went into the woods to get blueberries, currants, gooseberries, Juneberries, high-bush cranberries, and chokecherries. The garden had a surplus of vegetables such as potatoes, corn, and more. Occasionally we'd buy crates of peaches, apricots, and plums, and the Watkins [spice] salesman made his rounds on a schedule where we could buy ingredients. Plus we got cheese and ice cream at the creamery where Dad sold milk from our cows."

With a steady supply of fresh milk and flour bought in hundred-pound sacks for weekly bread making, pancakes were a regular treat in their household. "We could eat as many as we wanted," says Mary Lou.

They topped her mom's pancakes with butter and a syrup made by heating Watkins maple extract with some sugar. Homemade jelly or jam was always on the table as well, and leftover pancakes were often eaten as a snack with butter and sugar.

With pancakes this good, I am amazed there were ever any leftovers!

SERVES 4–6

2 cups flour

2 tablespoons sugar

1 teaspoon baking soda

1 teaspoon salt

2½ cups buttermilk (or sour milk: see tip)

1 egg, well beaten

1 teaspoon butter

for serving: butter, syrup, jam

Mix dry ingredients in a bowl. Add milk and egg; blend ingredients together. Batter will be a bit thick.

Heat a griddle or skillet until a few drops of water sizzle on the surface. Melt butter, then scoop batter onto the griddle, about ¼ cup for regular pancakes or about 1 tablespoon for silver dollar–size pancakes. Flip when batter starts to bubble, then cook until nicely browned.

Serve with butter, syrup, or your favorite jam.

tip To make sour milk, add 1 tablespoon vinegar or lemon juice per cup of milk. For this recipe, add approximately 2 tablespoons of either to 2¼ cups milk.

Baked French Toast

Shansel Biddle
Duluth, MN

the dish

French toast that's baked on a cookie sheet until golden brown and slightly crispy with a bread pudding–like texture.

the tell

This century-old recipe is the epitome of an oldie but a goodie. It comes from my husband's cousin Shansel, the keeper of their great-grandmother Maria's recipe for baked French toast. As the story goes, Maria made the French toast for her eight children before they set off on the walk to their country school near Roseau, Minnesota. According to the recipe card passed down to Shansel from her great-aunt Lenore, all the kids thought the French toast was delicious. Lenore notes, "Of course, at that time, Great-Grandma only had a wood stove." Yet she still managed to toast and butter each piece of bread before baking in a mixture of eggs, milk, and sugar until crispy and golden.

Shansel notes it's an easy recipe with only a few ingredients, yet so good. "I think it's a great recipe for Sunday brunch, possibly Christmas breakfast, or just anytime," says Shansel. "I love French toast!" The secret to its perfect texture is toasting the bread beforehand, which helps it absorb more of the custard while keeping the top golden and slightly crisp. The result is a baked French toast that is crispy on the top and edges and soft and custardy underneath, almost like a bread pudding.

This easy recipe makes for a simple yet satisfying dish. And I can see why Maria found it to be an efficient way to feed her small army of hungry children before they walked to school.

SERVES 4

8 slices bread

butter

8 eggs

3½ cups milk

3 tablespoons sugar

salt and pepper

Heat oven to 350 degrees. Toast bread and butter each slice on one side. Place the bread, buttered side up, in a single layer on a baking pan or rimmed baking sheet.

Beat eggs until nice and creamy; mix in milk and sugar. Stir in salt and pepper as desired. Pour mixture over bread. Let sit for 30 minutes so the bread can absorb some of the liquid. Bake for approximately 45 minutes, until custard is set.

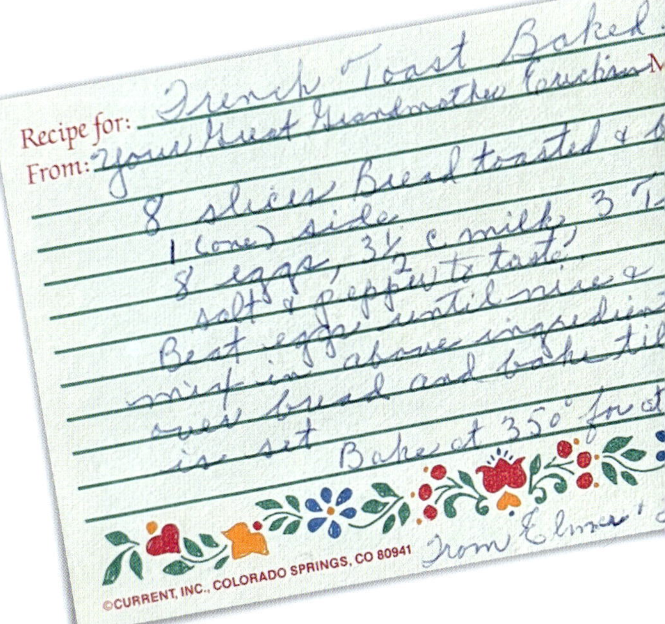
Recipe for: French Toast Baked
From: Your Great Grandmother
8 slices Bread toasted &
1 (one) side
8 eggs, 3½ c milk,
salt & pepper to taste
Beat eggs until nice &
mix in above
over bread and bake
is set Bake at 350°
©CURRENT, INC., COLORADO SPRINGS, CO 80941

Dutch Pancake

Julie Zeto
Bemidji, MN

the dish

A family-size pancake, baked until perfectly golden in the oven, with a custard-like center and irresistibly puffy, crispy edges.

the tell

More than forty years ago, Julie received this Dutch pancake recipe from a dear friend's mother. Since then, it has become a treasured family tradition, gracing her table for everything from special occasions to casual gatherings with friends. It's a dish she has returned to time and again—so much so that she included it in multiple cookbooks she has helped to compile for her church, Solway Lutheran, near Bemidji, Minnesota, a true testament to its timeless appeal.

Julie describes the Dutch pancake as the perfect choice for a celebratory breakfast, not only for its rich, buttery flavor but for its impressive presentation. "It looks special," she says. A simple dusting of powdered sugar and an array of toppings—strawberry sauce, butter, syrup—turn it into a showstopping centerpiece.

Also known as a Dutch baby or German pancake, this oven-baked breakfast item transforms humble ingredients—eggs, flour, and milk—into something spectacular. Poured into a sizzling, butter-coated skillet, the batter puffs dramatically as it bakes, yielding a pancake with a delicate, custard-like interior and crisp, golden edges—a perfect cross between a popover and Yorkshire pudding.

Julie acknowledges that, with only a few ingredients, it is a fairly easy recipe with one small exception. She says, "You have to act fast." Unlike some recipes that require letting the batter rest, this one is blended and poured straight into a preheated skillet containing melted butter to achieve the best rise and texture.

Julie suggests adjusting the recipe to different skillet sizes, ensuring flawless puffing every time. It's a tried-and-true favorite—proof that with just a handful of ingredients, you can create something truly extraordinary. »

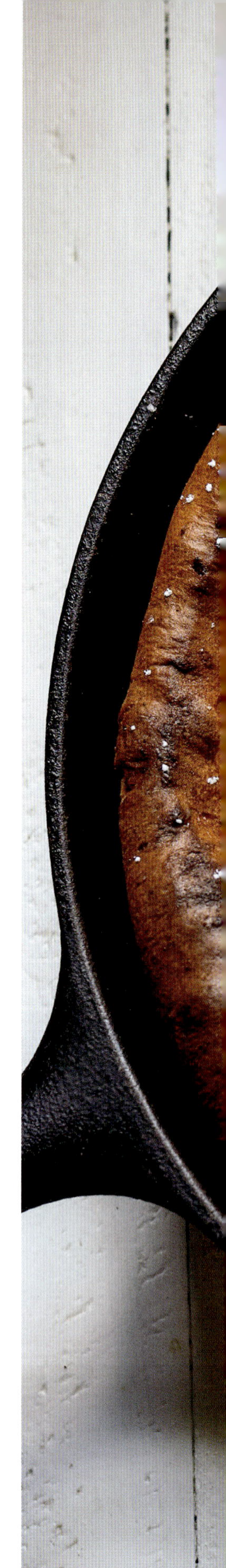

Dutch Pancake

SERVES 4–8, DEPENDING ON SIZE OF SKILLET

small (8-inch) skillet

4 tablespoons salted butter

3 eggs

¾ cup milk

¾ cup flour

medium (10-inch) skillet

⅓ cup salted butter

4 eggs

1 cup milk

1 cup flour

large (11-inch) skillet

½ cup (1 stick) salted butter

5 eggs

1¼ cups milk

1¼ cups flour

extra-large (12-inch) skillet

½ cup (1 stick) salted butter

6 eggs

1½ cups milk

1½ cups flour

topping suggestions

powdered sugar

lemon wedges

syrup or honey

fruit, hot fruit, or canned pie filling

Heat oven to 425 degrees. Have all ingredients ready to go; do not let batter sit after mixing.

Put butter in skillet or baking pan and place in oven. Meanwhile, mix batter with a blender or hand mixer. If using a blender, blend eggs at high speed for 1 minute, then, with the blender running, gradually pour in the milk and slowly add flour. Continue to blend for 30 seconds. If using a mixer, beat eggs until light and lemon colored, and gradually beat in milk and flour.

Remove the pan from the oven, pour batter into hot melted butter, and return to oven. Bake until puffy and well browned, about 20–25 minutes. Sift some powdered sugar on top and add your choice of toppings.

Note: The pancake will deflate a bit after removing from the oven.

just for fun Julie shared a tip: She uses her KitchenAid mixer to shred chicken. Simply add warm chicken breast that has been cut into pieces into the bowl of a stand mixer and mix on low.

Danish Puff

Megan & John Morrow
Minneapolis, MN

the dish

A people-pleasing pastry with a slightly sweet almond flavor that's a perfect complement to any holiday brunch spread or special occasion breakfast.

the tell

You know a couple is meant for each other when, unbeknownst to them, they grew up with a love for the same treasured brunch dish.

When Megan and John were dating and visiting Megan's family at Christmastime, John offered to make his family's special kringle. Megan recalls her surprise when she realized it was the same much-loved baked good that her family has eaten and adored for generations, albeit with a different name.

Megan's family has forever known the multi-textured pastry that is "light and flaky with a hint of sweetness and almond" as Danish puff. Her Grandma Cooper found the recipe in her Betty Crocker cookbook and soon discovered it was an instant hit among family and friends. She and her twin sister made it over and over again for various occasions from funerals to holidays to Sunday coffee, with additional members of the family continuing the tradition to this day.

John's family recipe hails from his mom's great-aunt Myrtle. Every year around the holidays, each sibling got to make a special Christmas request, and John's was always kringle, which he would make with his mom. Later in life, he frequently had to ask his sister for the recipe—until one year for his birthday his family had a picture of the original recipe card in their mom's handwriting imprinted on a carving board.

Megan appreciates that it's a recipe with simple ingredients she is likely to have on hand. However, one Christmas there wasn't almond extract in the pantry. She and John drove all over town to find the one open grocery store to secure the essential ingredient that gives this cherished family recipe its distinct flavor.

While Megan's family continues to call the pastry Danish puff, John's family still calls it kringle. "I don't think either of us is ever going to make the switch!" says Megan. No matter the name, both sides agree that it is beloved because it is so delicious and for all the sweet memories associated with it. ➸

Danish Puff

MAKES 2 LOAVES

pastry

1 cup flour

½ cup (1 stick) butter, at room temperature

2 tablespoons water

topping

1 cup water

½ cup (1 stick) butter

1 teaspoon almond extract

1 cup flour

3 eggs

glaze

1½ cups powdered sugar

2 tablespoons butter, at room temperature

½ teaspoon vanilla

1 tablespoon or more milk

chopped nuts or sliced almonds, optional

Heat oven to 350 degrees. In a bowl, combine 1 cup flour and ½ cup butter, using a pastry cutter or fork to blend until crumbly. Sprinkle with 2 tablespoons water, tossing with a fork until dough comes together. Shape into a ball, divide in half, and press into 2 (3x12–inch) rectangles on an ungreased baking sheet, leaving space between.

For the topping, in a saucepan bring 1 cup water and ½ cup butter to a boil. Remove from heat; stir in almond extract, then 1 cup flour. Cook over low heat, stirring until mixture forms a ball. Remove from heat, then beat in eggs until smooth. Spread topping evenly over rectangles.

Bake for 1 hour or until golden and crisp. Cool completely on a wire rack.

For glaze, mix powdered sugar, 2 tablespoons butter, vanilla, and enough milk for a spreadable consistency. Frost cooled pastry and sprinkle with nuts, if desired.

tips Topping the pastry with sliced almonds is a bit controversial on both sides of the family, says Megan, but the almonds can be a nice touch.

For added flavor, Megan's grandma put a splash of fresh-brewed coffee in the glaze frosting.

Megan suggests making a double batch as "it will still be gone before your brunch is finished."

For serving, slice the pastry crosswise into long pieces and serve on a platter.

just for fun Megan's Grandma Cooper was one of her biggest inspirations in the kitchen. "She was the best baker ever. Her pumpkin pie was delightful, her cookies were the freshest, and her 'slush' (a drink recipe that incorporated frozen Five Alive and fruit) is still missed today!"

Recipes
WISCONSIN
THE BADGER STATE
SUPERIOR
ASHLAND
HAYWARD
MERRILL
WAUSAU
ANTIGO
SHAWANO
MARINETTE
CHIPPEWA FALLS
EAU CLAIRE
STEVENS POINT
APPLETON
GREEN BAY
OSHKOSH
TOMAH
LA CROSSE
WAUPUN
MILWAUKEE
JANESVILLE
RACINE
AMERICA'S DAIRYLAND

Morning Sweets & Coffee Treats

Here's what's cookin'

Flatbread 33
Grandma Olson's Buttermilk Donuts 35
Swedish Almond Rusks 38
Grandma Helen's Cinnamon Coffee Cake Rolls 40
Sour Cream Somersault Cake 45
Cherry Nut Bread 46
Pumpkin Bread with Blueberries 48
Banana Bread 50
Poppy Kuchen 53
Grandma Drake's Apple Butter 55
Rhubarb-Orange Slice Preserves 58

On the best weekend mornings, I like to rise before the rest of my family so I can have a quiet kitchen all to myself and bake a special treat for them to wake up to. Typically it's banana bread or muffins, but some of my more ambitious endeavors include donuts and cinnamon rolls.

I savor the time alone, to focus on baking these "morning sweets" that are best enjoyed when gently easing into the day, often with those first cups of coffee. It's that time when you are not quite ready for breakfast but need a little something sweet to wake up your taste buds.

In fact, throughout my life coffee has signaled sweet treats. It's more than a drink to wake up with in the morning: Coffee is its own distinct meal occasion. Whether enjoyed in the morning or in the afternoon, coffee deserves a little something sweet to go with it.

My love of morning sweets and coffee treats surely comes from my parents, who always seemed to have baked goods to start the day. My mom used her toaster oven to warm up cinnamon rolls, Danishes, or coffee cake for my dad, who had the biggest sweet tooth of anyone I knew. When I would visit and see a little foil packet on the counter near the coffeepot, I'd get giddy in anticipation of what might be inside.

There is something about a warmed-up pastry, a butter-laden slice of some type of quick bread or flatbread, or another baked good served right from the oven that makes for better, sweeter mornings.

Flatbread

the dish

A thin and crispy, cracker-like bread best topped with a thick layer of butter.

the tell

Flatbread or flatbrød, its Norwegian name, was a special treat I enjoyed at my Grandma Hilma's house. Though Grandma Hilma didn't make it herself, it would arrive just in time for holiday gatherings, packaged in a large ice cream pail and delivered by the same woman who supplied my grandma with fresh, homemade lefse.

Unlike the cookies, bars, and sweet breads we eagerly devoured at Grandma's, flatbread was a rare, once-a-year indulgence, making it all the more special. At first glance it might seem like a dry, unassuming cracker, but slathered with butter it transforms into the perfect companion for morning coffee or afternoon tea—or, as I prefer, an all-day snack, conveniently left in a zip-top bag next to the butter dish during the holidays.

These days, I get my annual stash of flatbread courtesy of my mother-in-law, Mary Lou, who loves it as much as I do and grew up eating it as well. Her recipe, passed down from her mother, Charlotte, includes a touch of maple syrup, adding a hint of sweetness.

Mary Lou recalls that while her mom made flatbread for the holidays, she also made it throughout the year at the request of Mary Lou's Norwegian father, who enjoyed it with butter and a thin slice of cheese. Historically, flatbread was a staple among Norwegian farmers and peasants, often served with soups, fish, and meats. Because it's dry and free of moisture, it stores well for long periods, making it a practical, enduring tradition.

Today, many families with Norwegian heritage continue the tradition of flatbread. As Mary Lou says, "There are as many recipes for flatbread as people are making it." Her preferred method involves using a lefse grill and other lefse-making equipment as that is the way she learned to do it from a class she took many years ago. ➤➤

Flatbread

MAKES ABOUT 8 (10-INCH) ROUNDS

2 cups whole wheat flour

1 cup white flour

1 teaspoon salt

½ teaspoon baking soda

1 cup buttermilk

½ cup maple syrup

4 tablespoons butter, melted

Heat lefse grill to 350 degrees. Heat oven to 200 degrees. Combine dry ingredients in large mixing bowl. Add in wet ingredients and mix until dough is formed.

Portion dough into small balls. Take one at a time and roll out into a thin, 10-inch round on a lightly floured surface or pastry cloth.

Place each round on warm lefse grill or skillet (see tip) until it starts to brown, about 3 minutes; carefully flip and brown on the other side.

Place flatbread pieces on a cookie sheet and bake for about 2 hours or until the flatbread is crisp.

tips While you could roll out the flatbread on a flour-dusted counter and brown it in a skillet before placing it in the oven to crisp (see tip, right), Mary Lou likes to use her lefse tools, including a corrugated rolling pin and sleeve/cover, a pastry board with pastry cloth, a lefse grill, and a turning stick.

After rolling a portion of the flatbread dough into a thin piece, she places it on the lefse grill to brown on both sides before setting it on a cookie sheet to go into the oven (at a very low temperature) to crisp up—sometimes for two hours or more.

tip To make the flatbread without lefse equipment, roll out the dough balls into smaller rounds to fit the size of the skillet you will use to brown the flatbread pieces before baking.

Grandma Olson's Buttermilk Donuts

Jami Vandenberg
Lakeville, MN

the dish

A tasty morning treat, these buttermilk donuts are fried in a cast iron skillet for a just-right crispness on the outside while retaining a delicate interior.

the tell

Jami jokingly says these crispy donuts with a tender interior represent everything about her Grandma Olson all rolled into one. "My grandma could be a little hard on the outside but was soft and loving on the inside," says Jami, adding that this recipe has particular sentimental value to her. "Like everything my grandma made, the ingredients are simple and unassuming, but the best memories were created in the time spent making them."

Jami fondly recalls making the donuts when she'd visit her grandma, whose first name was Blanche, as a young girl. She was lucky to live near her grandma up until about third grade, just half a mile down the road in Wausau, Wisconsin, so they spent a lot of time together.

Sometimes it would be just her and Grandma making donuts. Other times aunts and other family members would join in the process of rolling, cutting, frying, and dipping. "Making donuts was a time when we all sat around the kitchen table taking on a task," says Jami. "The best conversation happened while donuts were being made." It could be a slow process but it was time well spent, catching up with family and working toward the ultimate payoff: fresh, homemade donuts dipped in sugar.

Some of Jami's other favorite dishes from her grandma's kitchen include fried chicken thighs, ham gravy, chicken noodle soup, and a signature item her grandma called "flutchies." These were made from leftover dough that wouldn't fit quite right in a loaf pan, so her grandma would fry them and put butter and sugar on them for a treat for Jami's dad and his siblings when they were growing up, and again in later years for Jami and her cousins. Jami says the flutchies are just one example of her grandma's resourcefulness, likely the result of raising five kids without a lot of money. "I'm amazed at what she could do with very little and how she saved and used EVERYTHING."

Jami adds that after her grandpa passed at the young age of fifty-six, her grandma remained in their home into her early nineties, so for many years she cooked only for herself unless family came to visit. Even on a limited budget, she perfected a few amazing meals and desserts to feed a crowd as the family grew over time to include Jami's four sets of aunts and uncles and ten cousins. "When we were there, we always requested the old favorites," says Jami. "Her focus was always on making what we wanted."

Today Jami continues the tradition of making homemade buttermilk donuts a few times a year with her daughter Eliza, usually on a day off or when they need a special homemade treat. She says, "It's something fun for me and Eliza to do together." »

When first making her grandma's recipe, Jami didn't have a donut cutter, so she and Eliza used a glass to cut the donuts and a star cookie cutter for the middles. When she shared a picture of their creativity on Facebook, one of her aunts, Connie, took notice and immediately sent her one of dozens of cookie cutters that had belonged to Jami's late aunt Patricia.

Jami's family clearly had a love for homemade donuts that they passed on to her, along with an appreciation for cooking and baking alongside loved ones. Jami also has many fond memories of baking with her mom, who used their time together as a teaching moment, helping Jami to learn fractions while making chocolate chip cookies. "Pretty much everything I've learned about baking and cooking came from my mom and grandma," says Jami.

Grandma Olson's Buttermilk Donuts

MAKES ABOUT 2 DOZEN DONUTS (OR MORE IF YOU LIKE SMALL DONUTS)

2 eggs

1 cup buttermilk

¼ cup vegetable oil, plus additional oil for frying

1 teaspoon vanilla

4 cups flour

1 cup sugar, plus more for rolling

4 teaspoons baking powder

¾ teaspoon salt

¼ teaspoon baking soda

In a large bowl, beat eggs until thick. Add remaining ingredients and stir thoroughly. On a floured surface, roll to half-inch thickness and cut with a donut cutter.

Fill a cast iron skillet about halfway with oil. Heat the oil to about 375 degrees; oil is ready when a drop of water sizzles in the pan. Add donuts, being careful not to overcrowd. When donuts look a bit golden, flip them and fry for another 2–3 minutes. Drain donuts on paper towel.

Optional: Roll in sugar or a cinnamon-sugar mixture.

Jami's kitchen advice

Clean as you go.

Divide sweet breads into two smaller pans so they bake more evenly.

Never trust the timer ... you just have to look at it.

tips

Dip the donuts in sugar right when they come out of the oil and are still hot.

The donuts are best eaten fresh, but a little zap in the microwave gives them life for a few days.

This recipe makes for great donut holes as well.

Swedish Almond Rusks

the dish

Rusks are a twice-baked, cookie–biscuit made with ground-up almonds for a subtle, not-too-sweet, nutty flavor. Great for dunking in coffee!

the tell

When I first encountered these oblong, cookie-like biscuits as a kid at my Grandma Hilma's house, I remember calling them "tusks," which makes sense as they kind of resemble an elephant's tooth.

Rusks, as the rest of the family called them, were stored in a plastic ice cream pail that would make an appearance at daybreak when the adults were having their first cups of coffee. Of course I didn't drink coffee back then, but I couldn't resist the opportunity to eat a cookie before breakfast, even if it had an odd shape and seemed a bit dry to my young taste buds.

I have since grown to appreciate rusks and their subtle, nutty flavor that comes from ground-up almonds. They are not overly sweet and their crisp texture makes them an ideal little morsel to dunk in a hot beverage, which is why I make them often to have on hand for morning (and afternoon) coffee.

Similar to biscotti, rusks are baked twice: once after rolling the dough into a large log shape, and then again after slicing, when those pieces are toasted on each side until they are golden brown. But while biscotti tend to include mix-ins such as nuts or dried fruit or may be dipped in chocolate, rusks rely on a shorter, less fussy ingredient list and are perfect in their plainness.

Rusks store well (in any type of resealable container, e.g., an ice cream pail) and are easy to wrap up and share with others as part of a care package with some nice coffee or an assortment of tea. I often source vintage biscuit jars from thrift shops and estate sales for just such occasions.

MAKES ABOUT 5 DOZEN

3 cups flour

1 cup sugar

1 cup ground almonds or almond flour

1 teaspoon baking soda

½ cup (1 stick) butter, at room temperature

½ cup sour cream, at room temperature

2 eggs

Heat oven to 300 degrees. Add all ingredients to large mixing bowl and mix well. Dump dough onto counter and divide into 4 equal portions. Form dough into rolls 9 inches long and 2 inches wide and divide between 2 cookie sheets.

Bake for 45 minutes or until light brown. Remove from oven, cool slightly, and cut into half-inch slices, aka rusks. Reduce oven temperature to 250 degrees and bake slices for about 15–20 minutes, then flip. Continue baking until rusks are light brown and crisp, another 15–20 minutes.

Almond Swedish Rusks
1 cup sugar
½ " butter or margarine
2 eggs
1 tsp soda
1 cup almonds ground (2¼ oz bag
½ " sour cream (dairy)
3 " flour if sticky add more
Put everything into mixing bowl
and mix well. Make 4 long rolls
across width of a cookie sheet
Bake at 300° for 45 minutes. When
light brown take out and cut in
½ inch slices. Toast first on one
side and then on other in a
250° oven until rusks are a
light brown and crisp (about
30-45 minutes in all

Grandma Helen's Cinnamon Coffee Cake Rolls

Shannon Thomasser
Prescott, WI

the dish

Old-fashioned cinnamon rolls with a cake-like texture that may be small in size but have an abundance of cinnamon and nutmeg flavor baked into every bite.

the tell

Shannon's love for homemade cinnamon rolls dates back to when she'd visit her grandparents' farm in Spring Valley, Wisconsin. Her grandma Helen, who lived to be ninety-eight, was an excellent cook and baker. "I remember walking into her house and looking to the kitchen table to see what goodies were made. We were pretty excited if these little rolls were there," says Shannon. "They were special because they were a homemade treat we only got when we went to visit my grandparents."

Like many dishes from past generations, there was no written recipe for the family-favorite cinnamon coffee cake rolls. Thankfully, Shannon had the chance to make them alongside Grandma Helen several years ago to learn the recipe and take copious notes. She is grateful for this time with her grandma, as they made a couple of recipes together and she now has these cherished family recipes in hand along with memories of that special day.

Observing her grandma in action was particularly helpful as Shannon picked up on some of the unique techniques that make these rolls so special. For instance, her grandma advised her to "sugar" the counter when punching out the cinnamon roll dough instead of using flour. Sugar serves a dual purpose, preventing sticking as well as adding a bit more sweetness and texture to the finished cinnamon rolls.

Grandma Helen also had a special method of folding the dough before cutting it into rolls. After patting the dough into a rectangle, she'd fold the top third to the middle of the rectangle (like how you'd fold a business letter) while pressing with the heel of her hand to seal. Then she pulled the lower left and right corners into the center, pressing to seal, repeating to create a little log, tucking the ends underneath and turning over the dough so the seam is on the bottom. Shannon believes this process allows for a more even distribution of the flavorful filling with less chance for leaking.

Baking alongside her grandma, she also got a lesson in working with fresh yeast versus dry yeast (see tips) and learned that it's perfectly OK to have a heavy hand with the nutmeg. "I think the nutmeg adds to the flavor of the cake rolls. Just a little something special," says Shannon.

Today Shannon's family continues to make homemade cinnamon rolls often, including each year on the Wednesday before Thanksgiving, when they deliver the welcome treat to neighbors, family, and friends. Her sons, Jonah and Jack, help in the process, and it has become a tradition they all look forward to each year. She says the best part is sharing and surprising people.

"It started as a special treat to have over the holiday when the boys didn't have school on Wednesday. These were not something we would have just any old weekend and not a Christmas treat but a Thanksgiving treat," says Shannon. "We enjoyed baking them together. Being that the boys were little and helping with the process, it was fun to share with others. Everyone would rant and rave about their work, and the boys just loved that. I liked being able to get the boys involved in the kitchen."

The boys, now grown, still help with the process to kick off the holiday season. Shannon admits they use a slightly different recipe for their big holiday bake, one she turned to when she couldn't find fresh yeast at her local grocery store and one that makes it a bit easier to turn out the cinnamon rolls in the large quantity they need to share. However, they often return to Grandma Helen's recipe to enjoy as a smaller group when it's just family.

"I eat those rolls and instantly am back at my grandparents' house as a kid," says Shannon. "Taste and smell are our time machine!"

Grandma Helen's Cinnamon Coffee Cake Rolls

MAKES 36 ROLLS

dough

about a half-inch piece fresh yeast, crumbled, or 1 (¼-ounce) packet active dry yeast dissolved in ¼ cup warm water (110 degrees) with ½ teaspoon sugar

½ cup water, warmed to 110 degrees

½ cup milk, warmed to 110 degrees

¾ cup sugar, plus more for rolling

1 teaspoon salt

1 teaspoon or more nutmeg

2 tablespoons butter, at room temperature

2 eggs, at room temperature

4 cups flour, plus more for kneading

filling

½ cup (1 stick) butter, melted and cooled to room temperature

½ cup or more sugar

1 tablespoon or more cinnamon

glaze

1 cup powdered sugar

about ⅔ cup heavy cream

If using active dry yeast, start by dissolving it in ¼ cup of warm water with ½ teaspoon sugar gently stirred in. Set aside for 5–10 minutes to let it bubble up before adding to the dough.

In a large bowl, mix together fresh yeast or yeast mixture, ½ cup warm water, milk, ¾ cup sugar, salt, nutmeg, 2 tablespoons softened butter, and eggs. Add flour; mix well.

Dust the counter with flour and gently knead the dough by hand. Note: This is a very sticky dough, but it will come together.

Generously grease a large bowl with butter; put the dough in the bowl and turn to coat in butter. Set in a warm place to rest for 45–60 minutes. Note: The dough doesn't rise much at all, so this is more of a "rest."

While the dough is resting, melt ½ cup butter and cool to room temperature. Heat the oven to 350 degrees; grease 1 (7x11–inch) or 2 (8x8– or 9x9–inch) pans.

Sprinkle the counter generously with sugar (yes, use sugar, not flour!). Place dough on the sugared counter and cut it in half. Flatten one portion of the dough and use your fingers to shape it into an approximately 6x18–inch rectangle (or as Grandma Helen suggested, "about as wide as your stretched hands, pinky to thumb"). Make sure you have plenty of sugar on the counter and on your fingers to keep the dough from sticking.

tips Use fresh yeast if you can find it as it gives the best flavor for these rolls; however, you can substitute with dry yeast.

Note: Fresh yeast cakes are 60 grams, and this recipe uses 20 grams or about a half-inch piece (⅓ of the cube).

If using instant dry yeast, use one packet or 2¼ teaspoons. Shannon says the rule of thumb is to divide by 3 when converting from fresh yeast to dry, e.g., instead of 30 grams of fresh yeast use 10 grams of dry.

tip Shannon grates her own nutmeg and says, "DON'T skimp on the nutmeg. It is what makes these rolls the best!"

To fold the dough, start with the top of the rectangle. Hold the two upper corners and fold to the middle of the rectangle (like folding a business letter). Then, starting at the bottom of the dough, hold the corners and fold the entire edge up and over the part you folded first. Repeat by folding the same way, to the middle from the top and then from the bottom, ending with the last fold to be rolled underneath the dough (you are rolling it into a tube).

Use your fingertips to make little divots on the top side of the tube—like dimples. Spoon the cooled butter over 0the dough and fill the dimples. Sprinkle the dough with ½ cup sugar, followed by cinnamon. Cut 1-inch-thick rolls and place cut side up in prepared pan.

Repeat the same process with the second half of the dough.

Before baking, spoon any extra melted butter over the cut rolls. Sprinkle with a little more sugar and cinnamon, which will yield a crunchy edge. Bake rolls on middle rack for 20 minutes or until the edges are golden brown. Tops should be a little browned, but still a cream color.

While the rolls are baking, make the glaze by mixing the powdered sugar and heavy cream in a bowl to desired consistency. Remove rolls from oven and drizzle with glaze.

fun food memories

Shannon recalls visiting her grandparents' house at Christmas when her grandma would bake all kinds of cookies and create impromptu cookie trays for anyone who stopped in for a cup of coffee. Each type of cookie lived in a Tupperware container or ice cream bucket and was stored on the steps going upstairs to the second floor (it was cooler there). Shannon says, "You would open the door to go upstairs and would be excited to see all those containers!"

Shannon shared another fun memory of when Grandma Helen made chicken-fried steak for family and friends who had to venture out one night to bring the cows back home after they got out. "No other chicken-fried steak has ever measured up!"

Shannon's kitchen advice

Wash up as you go. There are many times you are waiting for something to bake or to go to the next step in a recipe, and having soapy water ready saves time.

Shannon's mom taught her that you need to bring color and texture to your plate. Try not to have your meal be all one color. In other words: Include veggies!

Shannon's grandma taught her that you should always have something on hand to share with coffee if anyone stops in to visit.

Sour Cream Somersault Cake

the dish

A scrumptious coffee cake with sour cream as a star ingredient and layers of cinnamon sugar and nuts that create swirls of sweetness throughout the cake.

the tell

What's not to love about a cake with such a fun name? This coffee cake has been a staple in my mom's recipe box for over fifty years, passed down from a friend and cherished ever since.

Like many vintage cake recipes, it starts with a cake mix, which in my mind is a nice way to give yourself a leg up on a lazy weekend morning (or any time, for that matter). While some bakers prefer to make everything from scratch, I appreciate the ease and consistency that a good mix provides.

In addition to being a breeze to make, the cake has great flavor and texture thanks to the sour cream blended into the batter and the layers upon layers of cinnamon-sugar-nut mixture swirled in. Bake it in a Bundt pan and the result is a beautifully layered coffee cake that works as well for morning coffee as it does for an anytime dessert.

The original recipe from my mom's recipe box calls for an 18.25-ounce yellow cake mix, but today's standard cake mixes are typically 15.25 ounces. Over the years, many brands have adjusted their formulas to maintain the same results with slightly smaller packages—something to keep in mind when making older recipes.

Sour cream somersault cake has become a favorite at many of our family's brunch events through the years as well as a nice treat we enjoy with morning coffee when the occasion calls for it. I have even brought it on the road, for camping trips or weekend getaways, and it travels really well.

SERVES 12

butter to grease the pan

¾ cup sugar

2 tablespoons cinnamon

1 cup finely chopped nuts

1 (15.25-ounce) box yellow cake mix

1 (3.4-ounce) package instant vanilla pudding

4 eggs

1 cup sour cream

¾ cup water

¼ cup vegetable oil

1 teaspoon vanilla

Heat oven to 350 degrees. Grease a 10-inch Bundt pan with a heavy hand. Combine sugar, cinnamon, and nuts; use about a third of the mixture to cover the inside of the pan; save the rest for layering within the cake.

In a large bowl, blend together remaining ingredients for the cake batter. Alternate layers of batter in the pan with the cinnamon-sugar-nut mixture. Bake for approximately 1 hour, until an inserted toothpick or cake tester comes out clean. Cool well before removing from pan.

Wrapped in foil, this cake will last for several days.

Cherry Nut Bread

the dish

Pretty and pink thanks to maraschino cherries, this delicate sweet bread with a nostalgic flavor makes a nice gift to share with others or to have on hand for holiday entertaining.

the tell

Cherry nut bread is one of the special treats my mom made at the holidays and a few other times during the year. It stood out among her other goodies because of its pretty pink color and because my mom would bake it in soup cans, which resulted in adorable little round loaves featuring rings carved into the bread from the tin cans.

This bread's flavor reminds me of the cherry nut ice cream from Bridgeman's that was frequently in the freezer at my grandparents' house. I didn't love ice cream with nuts as a kid, but as an adult I crave this flavor and the nostalgia that goes with it.

My mom got the recipe from her cousin Arlene, who was an amazing baker and a huge influence on my mom. They grew up in Bemidji, Minnesota, not far from each other, and when Arlene got married and moved to the Iron Range my mom would visit in the summer to help care for Arlene's five children. My mom remembers watching Arlene work tirelessly in the kitchen, putting so much love into her cooking and baking. We think of Arlene whenever we make this cherished recipe.

MAKES 1 LARGE LOAF

½ cup (1 stick) butter, at room temperature

1½ cups sugar

3 eggs, beaten

2½ cups flour

2 teaspoons baking powder

pinch salt

½ cup milk

¼ cup cherry juice (from a jar of maraschino cherries)

1 teaspoon vanilla

½ cup quartered maraschino cherries

½ cup chopped nuts

Heat oven to 350 degrees. Grease and flour a 5x9–inch loaf pan.

In a large bowl, combine butter and sugar, mixing thoroughly; stir in beaten eggs.

In a separate bowl, sift together flour, baking powder, and salt; add to egg mixture and mix well. Stir in milk, cherry juice, and vanilla. Fold in cherries and nuts. Pour batter into prepared pan. Bake for approximately 45 minutes, until an inserted toothpick or cake tester comes out clean or with just a few moist crumbs.

tips I prefer to use toasted walnuts for this recipe. Simply place a skillet over medium heat, add walnuts, and toast, stirring occasionally, for 3–4 minutes. Remove the nuts from the skillet and chop as desired.

To bake this bread in soup cans, be sure to use cans that don't have a ridge at the top, which will make it more difficult to remove the baked bread. Lightly grease 4–5 cans and fill about halfway with batter. Place cans on cookie sheet to bake. Use a toothpick or cake tester to check for doneness at 30 minutes. Allow the bread to cool in the cans before sliding a knife around the edges to loosen and then gently removing the mini loaves.

Cherry Nut Bread

1/2 c. butter
2 1/2 c. flour
1/4 c. cherry juice
1/2 c. cherries, cut up
pinch of salt
1 1/2 c. sugar
3 eggs, beaten
2 t. b. pwd.
1/2 c. milk

1/2 c. nu
1 t. vanill

Pumpkin Bread with Blueberries

Sarah Hlusak
Plymouth, MN

the dish

Blueberries bring an unexpected yet delightful twist to this pumpkin bread, adding bursts of juicy flavor to a beloved classic.

the tell

My friend Sarah, who fancies herself more of a baker than a cook, tends to veer toward the tried-and-true recipes she had growing up—just one more reason I adore her! Among her most cherished family favorites is pumpkin blueberry bread, a recipe passed down from her mom. "It tastes AMAZING," says Sarah. "Very flavorful and unexpected to have blueberries in it, which make the taste even more incredible."

Her mom, Colette, received the original recipe from a friend more than fifty years ago, and it quickly earned a permanent spot in her recipe box. She often baked the bread in the empty pumpkin cans themselves, both large and small, leaving guests wondering how she achieved such a perfect form.

This kind of ingenuity was a hallmark of Sarah's upbringing. She was raised in Virgil, Illinois—farm country about an hour west of Chicago—and her family embraced a resourceful, homemade lifestyle. They canned their own food, grew produce, and even made sausage at her grandparents' farm just up the road. "Nothing went to waste back then," Sarah recalls.

She first started making this bread herself in college in the early nineties, often sharing it with study groups—an unusual habit for a student, but one her friends wholeheartedly appreciated. Today she continues the tradition, baking countless loaves to give as holiday gifts. "It's something my friends can't wait to receive," she says. "I make so many at once that I can only smell pumpkin for a week!" Not everyone in her household is thrilled about the holiday baking frenzy, though. "My kids aren't happy that most of the pumpkin bread disappears as soon as it's made. Our freezer is PACKED with it, and then—poof—it's gone, off to neighbors and friends."

MAKES 1 LARGE LOAF

- ⅓ cup vegetable shortening (Crisco)
- 1⅓ cups sugar
- 2 eggs, beaten
- 1 cup pumpkin puree
- 1⅔ cups flour
- 1½ teaspoons cinnamon
- 1 teaspoon baking soda
- ¼ teaspoon baking powder
- ¾ teaspoon salt
- ¼ teaspoon cloves
- ¼ cup blueberries

Heat oven to 350 degrees and lightly grease a 5x9–inch loaf pan.

In a large bowl, combine shortening and sugar, mixing well; stir in eggs and pumpkin. Mix in flour, cinnamon, baking soda, baking powder, salt, cloves, and blueberries. Pour into prepared pan and bake for 1 hour. Remove from oven and let cool for about 10 minutes before removing from the pan.

tips You can make muffins or loaves, but keep an eye on this bread in the oven because the size of the pan matters. A larger loaf will take about 1 hour, but smaller loaf pans or muffins take about 30 minutes. Sarah has even made this recipe in a Bundt pan.

Baking the bread in pumpkin cans gives the loaves a fun, round shape. Fill lightly greased tins just over halfway and use a toothpick or cake tester to check for doneness after 45–50 minutes. Allow the bread to cool in the cans before sliding a knife around the edges to loosen and then gently removing the mini loaves.

just for fun Sarah and her extended family all have a go-to cookbook, *Vittles from Virgil*. She says, "There's something nostalgic about the tight community that used to exist in a small town. I recognize the people in that book because we were all connected through church or church events."

Sarah's Kitchen Advice

"My mom taught me to roll with it! I have learned to eyeball things and get creative versus specific."

"The oven is a great place to store stuff because it's airtight. My grandma was a farm wife and had to cook for a family of eight kids. Whenever I went to her house, I knew I could find some sort of treat. She would always have a baked and frosted sheet cake in the oven for snacking."

Banana Bread

Janet Bromberg
Monticello, MN

the dish

This tried-and-true banana bread is perfect on its own or as the foundation for some flavorful add-ins. It can even be made gluten-free or in muffin form.

the tell

Everyone needs a go-to banana bread recipe—one that will be there for you when your blackened, too-ripe bananas are staring you in the face but are no longer desirable for eating on their own.

Janet's family-favorite recipe hails from a church cookbook she got back in 1979 when living in Lindstrom, Minnesota. Appearing on page 34 of Trinity Lutheran Church's *Minnesota Collectors Cookbook*, the recipe was submitted by someone familiar to Janet. "We knew the family who shared the banana bread recipe, so I knew my family would also like it," says Janet. "I still use it to this day." Janet says it's the only recipe she consistently has made over and over again and the only banana bread her family likes.

tips Sometimes Janet adds chocolate chips or walnuts (she avoids nuts if she's uncertain whether someone has nut allergies).

She says the bananas should be ripe but not mushy. She adds, "I put in more bananas than it calls for."

Janet says she bakes this bread more often in the winter as her husband hates to have her "heat up the house" by baking in the summer.

MAKES 1 LARGE LOAF, 3 SMALL LOAVES, OR ABOUT 18 MUFFINS

½ cup oil

1 cup sugar

2 eggs, beaten

4 bananas, mashed (about 2 cups)

3 tablespoons milk

½ teaspoon vanilla

2 cups flour, sifted

1 teaspoon baking soda

½ teaspoon baking powder

½ teaspoon salt

½ cup chopped nuts, optional

Heat oven to 350 degrees. Grease a 5x9–inch loaf pan, mini loaf pans, or muffin tin.

In a large mixing bowl, beat oil and sugar; add beaten eggs, mashed bananas, milk, and vanilla and mix well. Mix in flour, baking soda, baking powder, salt, and nuts (if using). Pour batter into prepared pan and bake for 20–25 minutes for muffins, 35–40 minutes for smaller loaves, or 1 hour for a large loaf. An inserted toothpick or cake tester should come out clean or with just a few moist crumbs.

just for fun When asked what the oldest thing is in her kitchen, Janet jokes, "It's me!"

Something she cherishes in her kitchen is a set of embroidered dish towels made by her mom.

A treasured memory: "My mom made all of our bread, and for special occasions she would cut an angel food cake into bar-sized pieces and cover them with powdered sugar frosting and roll them in chopped salted peanuts. Those times were special."

Sarah's notes

Add the nuts! I also like to throw in some chocolate chips or blueberries for a little twist.

This recipe can be made gluten-free. I tested it with Bob's Red Mill 1-to-1 Baking Flour.

Poppy Kuchen

Katie Nelson
St. Paul, MN

the dish

A German coffee cake with a luxurious layer of poppy seed filling that's topped with crumbly, buttery streusel.

the tell

In Katie's family, there are never too many cooks in the kitchen when it comes to baking poppy kuchen. It's a recipe that goes back to Katie's Great-Great-Grandma Janson and has been passed down through several generations, changing ever so slightly but remaining a beloved family favorite.

As the story goes, when the recipe was passed to Katie's great-grandma Laura Claessen, aka Grandma C, some in the family requested more poppy seeds. She obliged by increasing the quantity to a whopping two pounds (six cups) of poppy seeds for a recipe that yielded four large pans of poppy kuchen.

Baking in such large batches made sense, as poppy kuchen was a staple at church dinners, at holiday gatherings, and in family freezers—ready to be shared or gifted at a moment's notice. Grandma C's eight grandchildren were among the lucky recipients, eagerly awaiting her Christmas tins filled with poppy kuchen and gingersnaps, another of her signature treats.

Grandma C passed on the recipe to her daughter Margy—Katie's grandma—who, along with other family members, continued baking the cherished coffee cake in their own kitchens. That is until recently, when they made it their mission to prepare the family recipe together.

Under Grandma Margy's watchful eye, four generations gathered in the kitchen—Katie, her mom, Mary, aunts, cousins, and a few "little helpers." And just like that, a new tradition was born. "It was so fun to make poppy kuchen together," says Katie. "Ever since my great-grandma passed away, we'd bake it but not usually together. We've always wanted to and will definitely do it again." Beyond creating new memories with four generations coming together to bake poppy kuchen, Katie says it was helpful to bake alongside Grandma Margy and get some tips firsthand, such as paying attention to the dough to know when to add a little more flour if it isn't coming together or observing the designated scoop and spatula Grandma Margy prefers for this recipe.

Katie says her family typically enjoys poppy kuchen around the holidays, but it's a treat she looks forward to more often now as she has gotten older, as it's the perfect accompaniment to her morning coffee. "The recipe is sentimental to me and probably an acquired taste, biting into that much poppy seed, but it's so good!" says Katie. The recipe now has an added layer of meaning through making it together with family. She is thankful to her grandma Margy for keeping the tradition going and looks forward to making poppy kuchen with her family for years to come. ➤➤

Poppy Kuchen

MAKES ABOUT 3 DOZEN BARS

poppy seed filling

1½ cups poppy seeds

¾–1 cup milk

½ cup applesauce

1 egg, beaten

2 tablespoons flour

2¼ teaspoons butter, at room temperature

½ cup sugar

splash vanilla

streusel topping

1 cup flour

¾ cup sugar

½ cup (1 stick) butter

½ teaspoon vanilla

coffee cake

1½ teaspoons active dry yeast

¼ cup water, heated to 110 degrees

1 egg, at room temperature

¾ cup milk, heated to 110 degrees

3 cups flour

¼ cup sugar

½ teaspoon salt

½ cup vegetable shortening (Crisco)

for the poppy seed filling

Put poppy seeds and ¾ cup milk in blender and liquefy, adding more milk if needed. Blend for 1 minute. Add applesauce, egg, and 2 tablespoons flour and blend again until combined.

Transfer mixture to a heavy, 6-quart saucepan; stir in 2¼ teaspoons butter, ½ cup sugar, and a splash of vanilla. Heat to boiling over medium heat, stirring constantly to prevent scorching. Set aside to cool completely.

for the streusel topping

In a medium bowl, combine 1 cup flour, ¾ cup sugar, and ½ cup butter using a pastry cutter or fork until crumbly like pie crust. Stir in ½ teaspoon vanilla. Set aside.

for the coffee cake

In a medium bowl, dissolve yeast in ¼ cup warm water with a sprinkle of sugar; set aside to bubble up. Add egg and ¾ cup warm milk to yeast mixture, stirring to combine.

In the bowl of a stand mixer, combine 3 cups flour, ¼ cup sugar, and salt. Add shortening and mix until crumbly. Add in liquid ingredients and mix until dough comes together and lifts from the bowl. (You can also mix by hand.) Cover and let the dough rise for about 1 hour.

Preheat oven to 350 degrees. Dump dough onto 12x17–inch jelly roll pan and pat to fill the pan to its edges. Spoon the poppy seed filling over the dough and then sprinkle the streusel topping on top of the filling. Set aside to rise for about 15–20 minutes. Bake 25–30 minutes, until golden brown.

katie's kitchen advice

Get a digital kitchen scale. Katie says it's easy to operate and gives added confidence when measuring ingredients like flour. Her aunt, who works in the test kitchen for General Mills, says it's the only way to go.

tips

Buy poppy seeds in bulk at your local co-op or online. Katie's mom sources them from a restaurant supply company.

Make the poppy seed filling a day ahead: It needs to be blended, cooked to a boil, and cooled.

Poppy kuchen freezes well. Katie recalls that her grandma kept some on hand for gifting or church cakewalks.

Grandma Drake's Apple Butter

Jess Riepe
Twin Valley, MN

the dish

A century-old recipe, this apple butter starts with apples cooked low and slow to achieve a silky fruit spread that's perfect to eat on toast or straight from the jar.

the tell

Jess's family recipe for apple butter has truly stood the test of time. Resembling spiced applesauce but thicker like a fruit spread, this tasty treat originated with Jess's Great-Grandma Drake more than a hundred years ago, but the recipe took an interesting path to find its way back to Jess.

The journey started several years ago when her son Owen was getting ready to prepare his annual entries in the Food Preservation category for the Norman County Fair's 4-H competition. A fourth-generation 4-H participant, Owen started entering canned items in the fair at the age of eight. His first entry was a family recipe for salsa, but his passion soon evolved to unique flavors of jellies such as soda pop–flavored jelly (Mountain Dew, Dr Pepper), coffee jelly, and even one made from rose petals. "Because the motto of 4-H is 'to make the best better,' our family rule has always been to try something new each time," says Jess, meaning they never repeat recipes in the competition.

In 2018 Jess encouraged Owen to make apple butter, something she had enjoyed as a kid. When she put out a recipe request on Facebook, she was surprised when a neighbor replied and shared a recipe that was said to have come from Jess's aunt Kathy.

Owen made the recipe that year and earned a blue ribbon. Later that summer Jess and Owen took the surplus apple butter to a family reunion. Upon sharing it with family, they were surprised when Aunt Kathy informed them that the recipe originated with Jess's Great-Grandma Drake, who made apple butter every fall. Delighted to learn the recipe had even deeper origins in her family, Jess has made apple butter her annual tradition. Like her great-grandma, she uses crab apples but doesn't discriminate against other varieties, tapping her neighbors to ask if they have any extra fruit. She has used everything from crab to chestnut to snow to sweet as she tries to use up the apples nobody wants.

Her northeastern Minnesota community has a bounty of apple trees thanks to early arrivals who planted them in abundance. They recognized it would take only a couple of years until the trees produced fruit and they'd be on a path to make hard cider, not to mention other apple delicacies. "I guess we have the pioneers to thank for all the apples and the crab apple butter recipe," says Jess, who notes that some of her friends say it's the best they've ever had.

Of course Jess agrees and truly cherishes the recipe, even more so knowing of its origins in her family tracing back to her great-grandma. "Even though I never made the apple butter with my great-grandma or her daughter who is my grandma Donna, I am thankful to have her recipe and that this tradition is kept alive in the family thanks to a neighbor and 4-H." ➤

Grandma Drake's Apple Butter

MAKES ABOUT 6–8 PINT-SIZE JARS

8 cups cored and sliced apples (no need to peel)

4 cups sugar

1 cup water

½ cup apple cider vinegar

2 teaspoons cinnamon

pinch salt

Place apple slices in a slow cooker and cook uncovered on low for 8 hours.

Stir in remaining ingredients. Cook uncovered on low for 4–6 hours (up to 8 hours), until apples are dark brown.

Ladle mixture into a blender or use an immersion blender, food mill, ricer, or potato masher to pulp the apples. Spoon mixture into sterile containers, cover, and refrigerate or follow instructions for canning with a water bath (see page 58).

tips

While Jess's great-grandma's original recipe called for cooking the apples on the stovetop, it works very well in a slow cooker, uncovered on low. The longer the apples cook down, up to twelve hours, the better.

It's key to leave the cover off the slow cooker so the moisture can escape.

It's a versatile recipe in that you can cut it in half, use different varieties of apples, leave the peel on the apples, or just use the pulp. Jess notes that the peel contains all the nutrients!

Jess typically eats apple butter on toast but has been known to eat it straight out of the jar.

Sarah's notes

A pinch of cloves and a few splashes of vanilla can be nice additions for a flavor boost.

Add a few dollops of apple butter to the batter to sweeten homemade waffles or pancakes.

just for fun

Jess is lucky to have a vintage Oster Kitchen Center (an all-in-one appliance that can be used as a mixer, juicer, food processor, grinder, and more). She likes to use it to make apple butter because it has an "apple saucer/potato ricer" attachment. Jess says it "makes light work" as it spits out the seeds and peels and just leaves the pulp.

When Jess reached out to her family members for information on her great-grandma's apple butter and other recipes, she learned her aunt Sandy actually had her grandma's recipe box with several of her handwritten recipes, including one for Honey Jumbos that Jess had been searching for, for years.

Rhubarb–Orange Slice Preserves

the dish

Rhubarb combined with orange jelly candy makes for a marmalade-like topping for toast and crackers.

the tell

During rhubarb season, my mother-in-law, Mary Lou, makes the most delicious jam that includes an unexpected ingredient: little bits of orange candy—yes, those soft chewy, jelly candies with the sugar coating!

The vintage recipe for rhubarb–orange slice preserves comes from her mother, Charlotte. Mary Lou says the jam was a staple item to enjoy with breakfast toast or with morning coffee, although she and her brothers liked it specifically for the candy. "Adding the orange gummy candies to something that would be plain all of a sudden made it fancy," says Mary Lou. She recalls rhubarb being abundant at her family farm's garden and being used to make a host of seasonal menu items, from pies and breads to sauces for topping desserts. The recipe remains one of Mary Lou's favorite ways to use up her rhubarb; she cans several jars to store for the offseason or to share with friends.

MAKES 5 HALF-PINT JARS

4 cups finely sliced rhubarb

3 cups finely chopped orange slice candy (approximately 14 ounces)

1 cup sugar

2 cups orange juice

In a large saucepan set over medium-high heat, combine rhubarb and orange slices with sugar and orange juice. Bring to a slow boil, stirring constantly. Continue to cook about 20–30 minutes or until it reaches desired consistency. Spoon mixture into sterile containers, cover, and refrigerate. If you are planning to preserve for future use, follow Mary Lou's instructions for a water bath, below.

Water Bath Canning Method

Place empty jars (without lids or rings) in a canner or large pot with enough water to cover with an inch of water. Bring water to boil for a few minutes, then use a jar grabber to carefully remove and empty the jars.

Place brand-new lids in a small saucepan with hot, not boiling, water to soften the sealing compound. Keep them warm until needed.

Ladle preserves into sterile jars, leaving a half-inch of headspace and sliding a plastic knife or rubber spatula around the inside edges to remove air bubbles. Seal by adding hot lids and gently tightening rings around the lids (about halfway). Place covered jars back in hot water bath; boil for 10 minutes. Carefully remove and set upright on a towel-lined counter and cover with a dish towel; jars will seal as they cool.

tips For a test to see if the jam has set, place a plate in the freezer for 10 minutes. Remove the plate, spread some jam on it, and then slide your finger through it. If the jam doesn't run together, it should be good.

In addition to enjoying the preserves on toast, Mary Lou suggests spooning some over a layer of cream cheese on crackers.

Recipes

Iowa Ham Balls (1/2 receipe makes 11 balls)

3½ lbs. ground ham
1½ lb. ground beef
3 eggs, beaten
2 C. milk
3 c. graham crack. crumbs
2 Cans (10¾ oz. ea.) condensed tomato soup, undiluted
¾ c. vinegar 1c + 2T. 1½ rec.
2½ c. brown sugar
1 tsp. prepared mustard

In a large mixing bowl combine first 5 ingredients. Using a ⅓ c. measure, shape mixture into 2 inch balls. Place in 2 large shallow roasting pans.

Combine all remaining ingredients, pour over and bake at 325° for 1 hr. Basting frequently.

Memorable Mains & Sides

Here's what's cookin'

Juicy Lucy Tater Tot Hotdish 63
Ede's Meatballs 66
Ham Balls 69
Roast Beef & Pork with Gravy 70
Meatloaf Muffins 73
Iron Range Pasties 74
Succulent Sesame Chicken 76
Carol's Italian Shells 78

Homemade Noodles 80
Saltine Cracker Breaded Walleye 82
Dill Butter Carrots 85
Creamy Cucumbers 86

Not all memory-making meals are part of festive celebrations or are reserved for the holidays. Often it is the everyday dishes—the familiar and comforting foods shared over and over—that symbolize recipes from the heart and represent a memorable time when the family was gathered around the table.

Looking back at the list of daily home-cooked meals my mom made for my dad and that he logged for me in his final years, I see many of my favorite dishes that were in regular rotation at our family table when I was growing up. My mom's Italian stuffed shells with garlic bread, my aunt Ede's meatballs, and, of course, our Sunday dinners, which often consisted of roast pork and beef or roast chicken—always with mashed potatoes and my mom's glorious gravy.

Side dishes, too, had their place in our mealtime traditions. Dill butter carrots or creamy cucumbers may not have been the star of the table but still brought something special to the spread—a steady presence or a gentle reminder of a loved one who was known for a particular dish.

In talking with others about their mealtime memories, I often heard about treasured recipes like homemade noodles or pasties, where the act of preparing the dish is just as meaningful as the meal itself. Some of our most memorable meals aren't the grand feasts or special-occasion dishes but the somewhat humble, everyday ones made with love by the people we hold dear. These familiar dishes occupy a special place in our hearts and serve as a reminder that the feeling of home and togetherness is often found around the dinner table.

Juicy Lucy Tater Tot Hotdish

the dish

A tater tot hotdish twist on Minnesota's famous Juicy Lucy cheeseburger that is taste-test approved by a real-life Lucy.

the tell

We love our hotdish in Minnesota, especially when topped with crispy tater tots. But ope (!), this is not your ordinary tater tot hotdish. It's a twist on a Juicy Lucy—a cheeseburger made famous by a Minneapolis bar that includes hot, molten cheese that erupts from the middle of the burger instead of being placed on top. The burger is so legendary that I always wondered what it would be like as a hotdish—another iconic meal from our great state.

I had the chance to turn my vision into reality when the Minnesota State Fair announced a Minnesota-themed hotdish contest in 2021 as part of its annual blue-ribbon competitions. For two weeks leading up to the fair, I had several family members and friends over for hotdish tastings to provide feedback—including my daughter, Lucy. She was by my side as we tested different types of cheese and aimed for the perfect meat-to-pickles-to-tots ratio.

Lucy's Juicy Lucy Tater Tot Hotdish includes two layers of ground beef blended with caramelized onions, ketchup, mustard, and a beer-infused binder. In between these beefy layers is one of gooey American cheese as an ode to the recipe's namesake. All of this is topped with a row of dill pickle slices and, of course, tater tots. The "secret sauce" is the beer-infused binder. While most hotdishes involve a can of condensed soup, this homemade binder includes Grain Belt Premium American Lager, a trusty Minnesota beer, which gives it a great flavor—and who doesn't enjoy a Juicy Lucy with a pint of beer, anyway?

This elevated hotdish earned me a third-place ribbon in the Minnesota State Fair's hotdish competition, validating that a Juicy Lucy and tater tot hotdish combo is a winner. However, I admit that the real prize was partnering with my state fair sidekick and daughter Lucy to bring this new family-favorite recipe to life. »

Juicy Lucy Tater Tot Hotdish

SERVES 10–12

caramelized onions

2 tablespoons butter

1 large yellow onion, chopped

1 teaspoon sugar

1 teaspoon salt

¼ teaspoon pepper

beer-infused binder

2 tablespoons butter

2 tablespoons flour

½ cup milk

½ cup beer (e.g., Grainbelt Premium American Lager)

¼ teaspoon salt

¼ teaspoon freshly ground black pepper

hotdish

1½ pounds ground beef

⅔ cup ketchup, plus more for serving

2 tablespoons mustard

12 slices American cheese

1½ cups dill pickle burger chips, plus more for serving

1 (28-ounce) package tater tots

Step one: Caramelize the onions.

In a skillet, melt 2 tablespoons butter over medium heat. Add onion and sugar, 1 teaspoon salt, and ¼ teaspoon pepper. Cook for about 20 minutes, stirring occasionally and adding water throughout, a couple tablespoons at a time, to keep the onions from burning. Remove from pan and set aside.

Step two: Make the beer-infused binder.

In the same skillet, melt 2 tablespoons butter, slowly whisk in the flour until smooth, and continue cooking for a couple of minutes. Slowly whisk in the milk and beer and keep whisking until the sauce is thick and bubbly, about 5 minutes. Stir in ¼ teaspoon salt and ¼ teaspoon pepper and set aside.

Step three: Make the filling.

Heat oven to 350 degrees. In a large skillet, cook the ground beef until meat is no longer pink; drain off the fat. Mix in ketchup, mustard, caramelized onions, and beer-infused binder.

Step four: Assemble the hotdish.

Lightly grease a 9x11–inch casserole dish. Lay a base of half of the beef mixture. Add a layer of cheese singles. If you like it really cheesy, add two layers! Add the remaining beef mixture on top. Add a layer of pickles, then top with tater tots.

Bake for approximately 50 minutes, until tots are golden brown. Let stand for 15 minutes before serving. Garnish with ketchup and extra pickles.

Ede's Meatballs

the dish

Ordinary pantry ingredients make for extraordinary meatballs with luxurious golden mushroom gravy.

the tell

This is yet one more tried-and-true dish courtesy of my aunt Ede, who was known for creating delicious, comforting meals without too much fuss. She knocked it out of the park with this one.

Ede's meatballs may rely on standard pantry ingredients like evaporated milk and condensed soups, but they are anything but ordinary—just like Ede herself. After she passed away, I inherited Ede's old photographs and slides, uncovering aspects of her life I never knew. Beyond being a devoted schoolteacher and the ultimate homemaker, she had a passion for travel—venturing to Norway and other parts of Europe—and was a true artisan in quilting, as seen in the many photos of her intricate creations adorning her bedroom.

But the one talent our family always recognized was Ede's special way of making people feel welcome, often through the food she served at her cozy homes in Silver Bay, Cass Lake, and later in Bemidji, Minnesota. These meatballs in particular remain a favorite of many in our family, including my aunt Jean, who says, "These are always a big hit with company!"

Featuring golden mushroom soup as one of the star ingredients, the gravy for these meatballs is so good that my mom has been known to double the gravy portion of the recipe to have extra for mashed potatoes. I think Ede would approve.

My mom often served Ede's meatballs for Sunday dinner. When I make them now, I am immediately brought back to memories of those dinners with my parents and of my sweet aunt Ede.

MAKES 48 MEATBALLS; SERVES ABOUT 20

3 pounds ground beef

7 slices bread, cubed

1½ cups evaporated milk

1½ teaspoons baking powder

1 tablespoon parsley flakes

½ teaspoon salt

¼ teaspoon pepper

3 tablespoons flour

1 cup cold water

1 (10.5-ounce) can cream of onion soup

1 (10.5-ounce) can French onion soup

2 (10.5-ounce) cans golden mushroom soup

Heat oven to 350 degrees.

In a large bowl, combine ground beef, bread, evaporated milk, baking powder, and seasonings and use your hands to mix. Shape into 1½-inch meatballs and place in 9x13-inch pan.

Mix flour with cold water by shaking in a jar or whisking in a large bowl, then blend with the soups. Pour mixture over meatballs. Bake uncovered for 1 hour.

Ham Balls

the dish

Super-sized, sweet, and tangy meatballs made from ground ham and beef and crushed graham crackers.

the tell

From my first encounter with ham balls, at my friend Toni's wedding, I was smitten. It was the same wedding that also featured sandwich loaf (see page 118). Thinking back, that occasion was a pivotal food experience, as both dishes have been a part of my life ever since.

No surprise: Weddings and other big life moments often put the spotlight on family favorite foods and include recipes that are truly from the heart. This sentiment rang particularly true for my friend's wedding, where her aunts and relatives lovingly prepared many of the components of the celebratory meal.

Ham balls—often called Iowa ham balls—are larger than the average meatball. Bigger than a golf ball but smaller than a baseball, they are made with ground ham (not pork) and beef and crushed graham crackers, then topped with a sweet, tangy glaze that caramelizes in all the right ways while baking in the oven.

Some people make them as a way to use up leftover ham, but I prefer to skip the ham dinner altogether and go straight to my butcher's counter to ask for ground ham to make these delightful delicacies.

MAKES ABOUT 45 HAM BALLS; SERVES ABOUT 20

3½ pounds ground ham

1½ pounds ground beef

3 eggs, beaten

2 cups milk

3 cups graham cracker crumbs (about 3 sleeves)

2 (10.5-ounce) cans condensed tomato soup

¾ cup vinegar

2½ cups packed brown sugar

1 teaspoon prepared mustard

Heat oven to 350 degrees.

In a large mixing bowl, combine ham, beef, eggs, milk, and graham cracker crumbs, using your hands to mix well. Use a ⅓ cup measure to shape mixture into 2-inch balls. Place meatballs in a large, shallow roasting pan.

Combine tomato soup, vinegar, brown sugar, and mustard, stirring well, and pour over meatballs. Bake for 1 hour, basting frequently.

tips This recipe makes a large batch of meatballs, perfect for a potluck or holiday celebration. I often cut the recipe in half when I make them for a family dinner.

Ham balls freeze nicely: Make a big batch and then you have leftovers to look forward to.

Sunday Dinner
Roast Beef & Pork with Gravy

the dish

The simplest of recipes for tender beef and pork roast that, when made together, yields the most glorious, flavorful gravy.

the tell

Waking up to the scent of meat roasting on a Sunday was a familiar occurrence when I was growing up. We tended to have an early dinner, at noon or before, which meant my mom, Carol, would put the meat in the oven first thing in the morning and the smell would radiate through the house as I drifted in and out of sleep. Without fail, I would be just rolling out of bed when I was summoned downstairs for dinner, having slept right through breakfast.

I didn't appreciate waking up to such a hearty meal in my teenage years, but I have since grown to crave my mom's Sunday dinner. In addition to a platter of roasted meat, the meal always included a simple salad made of iceberg lettuce and French dressing, scalloped corn, fluffy mashed potatoes, and the BEST gravy—perhaps one of my mom's greatest culinary accomplishments.

There is something special about a mom's or grandma's gravy. It's consistently delicious with good flavor, always the right shade of brown, and never lumpy. It wasn't until I watched my mom make her Sunday dinner from start to finish that I learned I could perhaps achieve the same greatness.

My mom's secret is to roast a beef chuck roast and a pork roast together to get a more flavorful gravy. It's such a simple recipe that it's almost a "no-recipe" but results in fork-tender, flavorful meat. She starts by browning the meats in some oil and then puts them in her "special" roaster, a heavy-duty aluminum pan she claims roasts the meat to the perfect texture every time. From there, it's pretty hands-off until the meat is done roasting and it's time to make the gravy. This is when the magic happens.

My mom made these final moments in the preparation of Sunday dinner look effortless, but anyone who has made a big meat and potatoes dinner or prepared the Thanksgiving feast knows that the last few steps are a highly orchestrated event where timing is everything. While Carol was tending to the gravy—loosening up the browned bits in the roaster, adding water, whisking up a roux—she'd simultaneously mash the potatoes that had been peeled earlier that morning and timed to finish boiling just moments before serving. This same flurry of activity was on repeat each Sunday, and my dad, brothers, and I knew to steer clear to let Mom move about in her small but efficient galley kitchen and that we'd soon be rewarded with another delicious dinner.

Seated at the table, we'd patiently nibble on our salads as my mom put the final touches on the main dishes and carried them out one by one to be immediately passed around even before she'd take a seat. First there was the platter of pork and beef, next came a bowl with a mountain of mashed potatoes, and then the grand finale, which cued a sigh of relief and signaled we could all start eating (and that my mom could sit down)—the glorious gravy! ➻

Roast Beef & Pork with Gravy

SERVES 4–6, WITH LEFTOVERS

2–3 tablespoons oil

1 (3-pound) boneless chuck roast

1 (2- to 3-pound) boneless pork shoulder or pork loin

salt and pepper

⅔ cup flour

1⅓ cups water

Heat oven to 325 degrees.

Heat oil in a large skillet over medium heat. Brown the chuck roast on all sides and set aside; repeat with the pork roast. Put both meats in a roaster and sprinkle with salt and pepper. Cover and put in oven for about 3 hours.

Halfway through cooking, check to make sure there are juices in the roasting pan; if not, add some water.

When meat is fork-tender, remove from roaster and place on a sheet pan or in a 9x13–inch pan and cover with foil. Leave all juices behind in the roaster.

To make the gravy, add about 2 cups of water (see note) to the roasting pan, place on stovetop over low heat, and stir to loosen up all the crusty bits stuck to the pan.

In a separate container (for example, a Mason jar), mix flour with 1⅓ cups water. Gradually add the flour mixture to the pan while whisking constantly until desired consistency. You may not need to use all of the flour and water mixture.

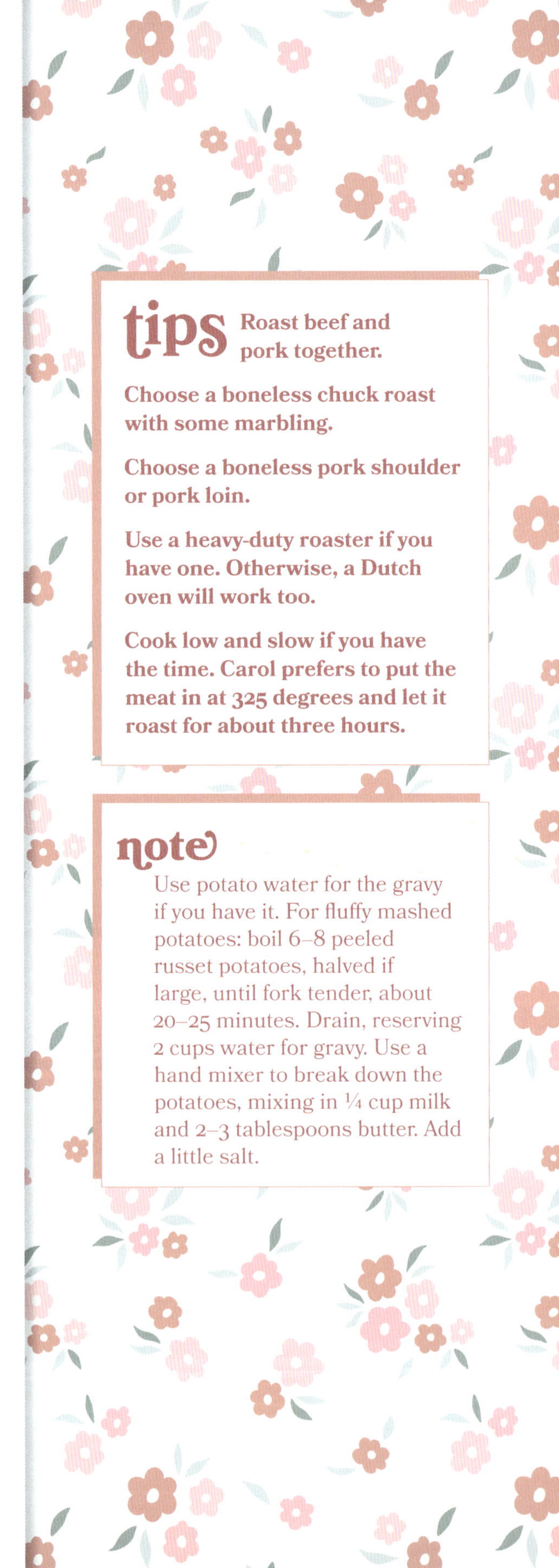

tips

Roast beef and pork together.

Choose a boneless chuck roast with some marbling.

Choose a boneless pork shoulder or pork loin.

Use a heavy-duty roaster if you have one. Otherwise, a Dutch oven will work too.

Cook low and slow if you have the time. Carol prefers to put the meat in at 325 degrees and let it roast for about three hours.

note

Use potato water for the gravy if you have it. For fluffy mashed potatoes: boil 6–8 peeled russet potatoes, halved if large, until fork tender, about 20–25 minutes. Drain, reserving 2 cups water for gravy. Use a hand mixer to break down the potatoes, mixing in ¼ cup milk and 2–3 tablespoons butter. Add a little salt.

Meatloaf Muffins

the dish

A fun-size version of my mom's meatloaf that makes for perfect portions and a faster cooking time.

the tell

Meatloaf doesn't always get the love it deserves. Maybe it's the name, or perhaps it's the frumpy appearance? However, I believe this hearty comfort food which is often backed with deep feelings of nostalgia is an unsung hero of easy weeknight meals. When made in individual muffin-size portions, it's a true game changer. And, dare I say, cuter in its presentation?

My love for meatloaf started with my mom's recipe from her prized *Pillsbury Family Cookbook*, a wedding shower gift in 1967. It's a traditional meatloaf that's topped with a tasty, sweet glaze made of brown sugar, vinegar, dry mustard, and Worcestershire sauce. It was in our family's regular rotation of weekday meals growing up and something my mom made quite often for my dad when they were empty nesters.

When my kids were young and I was looking for ways to make mealtime more fun, I started making meatloaf muffins. It was my feeble attempt to make this humdrum meal a bit more enticing and exciting—and it seemed to work!

Even though my kids are now adults, this dish in the individualized portions remains a family favorite. Making meatloaf in a muffin tin not only cuts down the cooking time but also makes portioning a breeze. Plus, let's be honest: When topped with mashed potato "frosting" and pea "sprinkles," these meatloaf muffins are pretty darn cute.

MAKES 12 MUFFINS

meatloaf

2 pounds ground beef

1 cup quick-cooking oats

¾ cup milk

¼ cup chopped onion

1 egg, lightly beaten

1 teaspoon salt

1 teaspoon Worcestershire sauce

¼ teaspoon pepper

glaze

½ cup packed brown sugar

¼ cup vinegar

1 teaspoon Worcestershire sauce

½ teaspoon dry mustard

for serving: mashed potatoes and peas, optional

Heat oven to 350 degrees. Combine meatloaf ingredients, mixing well, and scoop into cups of muffin tin, filling loosely.

In a separate bowl, blend glaze ingredients. Spoon glaze on the meatloaf in each cup.

Bake for 20–25 minutes. Remove mini meatloaves from the muffin pan (there will likely be some liquid that has pooled in the cups) and place on a baking sheet or serving dish. Optional: Top with mashed potato "frosting" and pea "sprinkles."

Iron Range Pasties

Meittunen Family
Hibbing, MN

the dish

Hailing from Cornwall, England, and making their way to the Iron Range, these savory handheld pastries are filled with beef, potatoes, onion, and, yes, rutabaga.

the tell

Pasties used to pop up in my house during childhood when various groups sold them for fundraisers in my hometown. I always loved the flaky pastry with its comfort food filling of meat and potatoes and the distinct flavor of rutabaga—which can be a controversial inclusion but is a hallmark ingredient of the traditional Iron Range pasty that came with the Cornish immigrants who settled in the area beginning in the late 1800s. I knew if I was going to share a pasty recipe in this book it had to be from a true Iron Ranger, and I knew just where to go.

One summer when I was camping at McCarthy Beach on Side Lake just north of Hibbing, Minnesota, I came across a cookbook for sale in the state park's office titled *Let's Party: Recipes, Stories & Silliness from Minnesota's Iron Range Recipe Diva and Former Go-Go Dancer*. This was my first introduction to Mona Meittunen Abel, a lifelong and very proud Iron Ranger, and I was smitten. I read Mona's entertaining cookbook cover to cover in one afternoon. Beyond many great recipes, it included "assorted sordid stories" from her life on the Iron Range. The self-proclaimed mayor of Side Lake, she chronicled her fascinating life as the oldest of six kids in a Finnish/Celtic family with many silly antics as well as interactions with celebrities from Bob Dylan to Tiny Tim. She was a true character, a bit of a prankster who lived life to the fullest and was always at the center of any gathering. I truly believe she could be the subject of her own movie.

The cookbook, which was one of five Mona had written, includes recipes for entertaining at the lake (preferably on a pontoon), foods that were customary at her family gatherings and holidays, and ethnic delicacies—including pasties. Mona shared a story about how a prominent food columnist from the *New York Times*, Molly O'Neill, visited Mona at her house for an interview and to share a pasty meal. Mona's family recipe for Iron Range pasties was included in O'Neill's book, *One Big Table: A Portrait of American Cooking*.

Side note: Perhaps most impressive is that nearly one-third of Mona's cookbook is devoted to tasty beverages, including classics like brandy Alexanders or grasshoppers and others with cheeky titles like Sex on a Snowbank or Lethal Weapon, where she says, "Use your imagination for amounts of vodka, peach schnapps, cranberry juice and a dash of lime juice."

No doubt it would have been a blast to meet Mona, but unfortunately she passed away in 2021 at the age of eighty. Through some dumb luck (and the internet) I realized Mona and I had a common friend, who put me in touch with one of Mona's sisters, Patti, who shared some additional insight on Mona's life and their family's pasty recipe.

Patti told me their grandmother Edith's family immigrated to the Iron Range from the Isle of Man in England, and their grandfather Jack's family was from Cornwall, where many believe pasties originated. Cornish miners on the Iron Range would take pasties, which are very portable and easy to eat, to work to eat in the mine. "Pasties are so handy to eat at any time," says Patti. "It's a whole meal in your hand."

Pasties soon became a staple of regional cuisine and eventually were an integral part of church fundraisers throughout the area. Patti and Mona's grandmother Edith and their mother, Myra, put in countless hours to make pasties to help support Wesley Methodist Church in Hibbing. Eventually Patti and Mona also chipped in to keep the fundraising effort going, with Mona purchasing additional equipment to help with the prep work. However, Mona shared in one of her cookbooks that eventually she turned in her apron, saying, "The 5 a.m. start time and going to work smelling like a pasty didn't work."

Thankfully, Mona went on to share her love of pasties with her family, friends, and cookbook readers, inspiring a new generation of pasty makers. "I love the family tradition and the history passed down," says Patti, who confirms the practice of pasty making is still alive and well among her relations today. From her sister-in-law, who makes dozens for the deer hunters in their family each fall, to her daughter, who makes appetizer-size pasties, to her brother, who brought the tradition to his home in Texas, Patti notes they are "prolific pasty people!"

tips Some pasty recipes may use butter or Crisco instead of lard, or hamburger instead of round steak, but Patti's mom, who was "persnickety about ingredients," used to say, "It's sacrilegious to use hamburger and Crisco."

The technique for crimping pasties takes a little practice, but Patti describes it as "grab, pinch, pull, and push forward with index finger."

Have fun with the shape and size: Patti's mom used to make pasty "pies" and her daughter makes an appetizer size.

MAKES 6

pastry

4 cups flour

1 tablespoon salt

8 ounces (1 cup) lard

about 1 cup cold water

filling

2 large russet potatoes, peeled and cut into half-inch cubes

1 pound round steak, cut into half-inch cubes

1 large onion, chopped

½ rutabaga, grated

6 teaspoons butter

salt and pepper

Heat oven to 400 degrees.

In a large bowl, combine flour and salt, then use a fork or pastry cutter to cut in lard until mixture is the size of peas. Stir in approximately 1 cup of cold water until dough is slightly sticky, using your hands if preferred. Divide dough into 6 pieces. Dust counter and rolling pin with flour and roll each piece into a circle the size of a dinner plate.

On one side of each dough round pile ½ cup potatoes, ½ cup meat, and portions of onion and rutabaga. Top with 1 teaspoon butter. Sprinkle with salt and pepper. Dampen edge of round with your hands or a pastry brush and fold one side over the filling. Press down carefully and crimp or flute edges to seal tightly.

Set on a sheet pan and bake for 15 minutes, then reduce temperature to 375 degrees and bake for 45 minutes or until pasties are golden brown.

Succulent Sesame Chicken

the dish

Juicy, tender chicken topped with a buttery sesame cracker crumb.

the tell

Growing up, certain dishes were reserved for company, and this was one example. Whenever my mom made this particular chicken dish, we knew guests were coming—grandparents, neighbors, or family friends.

I loved those evenings, which included a pretty table and lit candles. There was a buzz of excitement, the anticipation of who'd be joining us—hopefully, there'd be some kids to play with—and the promise of special dishes my mom would prepare. She loved to entertain, and cooking for others seemed effortless for her. The meals were simple yet always delicious.

Today, making this chicken myself, I understand why it was one of my mom's go-to dishes for company. It's a recipe that doesn't take too much effort yet results in a rich and indulgent dish that is oh-so-buttery. I particularly love all the scrumptious crumbs sitting atop the fork-tender meat. Not your typical weeknight chicken, it's worthy of a special occasion and meant to be shared.

SERVES 4–6

⅔ cup butter

1 tablespoon lemon juice

1 cup crushed sesame crackers

1 teaspoon garlic salt

½ teaspoon pepper

2½–3 pounds chicken (about 8 pieces)

2 tablespoons chopped parsley

Heat oven to 350 degrees. In a small saucepan set over medium heat, melt butter; add lemon juice and stir to blend.

Combine cracker crumbs, garlic salt, and pepper in a shallow dish.

Dip chicken in melted butter and roll in crumb mixture. Place chicken in an ungreased 9x13–inch pan. Sprinkle with remaining crumbs. Reserve remaining butter.

Bake for approximately 1 hour. Add parsley to the reserved melted butter and pour over the chicken. Return to oven for 5–10 minutes. Spoon melted butter over chicken and serve.

tip I make half of this recipe gluten-free by using gluten-free crackers for the crumb topping. Breton makes a great gluten-free cracker seasoned with herbs and garlic.

Carol's Italian Shells

the dish

Jumbo pasta shells stuffed with sweet Italian sausage and provolone cheese, then baked in spaghetti sauce.

the tell

Everyone has a favorite meal that tastes like home, and for me that meal is my mom's Italian shells. What's not to love about big pasta shells overflowing with a mixture of sweet Italian sausage and creamy provolone cheese and topped with hearty spaghetti sauce?

This is the dish our family asked my mom to make for birthdays, potlucks, and celebrations of every kind—always accompanied by her homemade garlic bread. And it's the dish I now make for my kids at their request several times a year. It's just as good for a weekday meal as it is to bring to a party or to share with others.

That's just what my mom did. Through the years, when she wasn't making shells for our family, it became her signature dish to share with neighbors celebrating a new baby, friends who just lost a loved one, or others who may not be up to cooking.

The recipe was shared with my mom in the early 1970s at a friend's house in Cloquet, Minnesota. My parents' group of teacher friends often gathered for dinner, drinks, and cards, and that night the hostess—who had roots on the Iron Range, a region known for Italian immigrant influences—served these shells. And the rest is history!

My mom has tweaked the recipe over time, perfecting it with her favorite ingredients. Making this dish with her is one of my most cherished traditions. In cooking together, I've learned that a recipe goes beyond instructions: It's about the little touches, the right ingredients, and the love that goes into it.

SERVES 8–10

24 jumbo pasta shells

1½ pounds Italian sausage (see tip)

1 tablespoon dried basil

1 tablespoon dried oregano

1 tablespoon Italian seasoning

1 clove garlic, minced

2 (16-ounce) jars spaghetti sauce

3 slices bread, torn into half-inch pieces

8 ounces provolone cheese, cut into quarter- or half-inch cubes

1 egg

1 cup shredded Parmesan or four-cheese blend

Heat oven to 325 degrees. Cook pasta shells according to package directions; drain and set aside. Brown the sausage and set aside to cool.

Combine spices and garlic with spaghetti sauce, stir well, and set aside. In a separate bowl combine sausage, bread, provolone cheese, egg, and ½ cup of spaghetti sauce.

Spread approximately ¾ cup of sauce in the bottom of a 9x13–inch pan. Stuff pasta shells with meat/cheese mixture; place in pan. Top shells with a generous amount of sauce; sprinkle shredded cheese on top. Cover with foil and bake for 1 hour.

tips My mom prefers the tender texture of Johnsonville Sweet Italian Sausage Links (casings removed) for this recipe.

To enhance the flavor of the spices, Carol rubs them in the palms of her hands before she adds them to the sauce and then runs it all through the blender.

The process of stuffing the shells can be tedious, particularly if you are making a double batch. My mom and I like to sit at the dining room table or at a card table in the living room while we work so we can take our time and enjoy being together.

Homemade Noodles

Cathleen Jones
Cambodia (formerly of Cokato, MN)

just for fun

Cathleen has made a handwritten cookbook of family-favorite recipes for each of her kids.

One year, her oldest daughter made special Christmas ornaments with a family recipe in her grandmother's handwriting on each side.

Cathleen's mom, Charlotte, who is the family historian and has done a lot of genealogy, has been a big influence on Cathleen's interest in family recipes, photos, and mementos.

the dish

Easy homemade noodles with only three ingredients.

the tell

Cathleen, originally from Cokato, Minnesota, grew up eating homemade noodles—a recipe passed down through the generations and rooted in tradition and nostalgia.

It started with her grandma Mildred, who lived on a farm in Moose Lake, Minnesota, and loved her poultry, raising everything from chickens and ducks to geese and guinea hens. In those days, making homemade noodles wasn't a rare treat—it was likely a practical, economical way to stretch a meal, especially with a busy farm to manage. "The noodles were always served in chicken or turkey soup, [made] using the leftover carcass and meat from roasting the bird," Cathleen recalls. "Making noodles was always part of the process. It was just what you did back then."

Eventually her grandma passed on the recipe to her daughter-in-law, Cathleen's mother, Charlotte, who continued the tradition even when she was working away from home. She would prepare and roll out the dough, wrap it in plastic, and leave it in the fridge for Cathleen to make when she got home from school. "I would heat the soup to bubbling, cut the rolled-up dough, and unroll each noodle before dropping into the soup," says Cathleen.

Even after Cathleen moved to Cambodia, where she has lived for more than thirty years, homemade noodles remained a fun tradition she has continued with her seven kids and six grandkids. In their kitchen, thousands of miles from Minnesota, the familiar process of rolling, cutting, and dropping noodles into bubbling broth became a beloved family ritual, connecting past and present across generations and continents. "My kids loved to help me make noodles and especially liked dropping them into the soup. They often helped to do the rolling and cutting, so our noodles were always oddly shaped. We didn't care: They still taste great!"

Today Cathleen still makes the noodles, but they've become more of a special occasion food. She has taught her own daughter-in-law, Sona, who is Cambodian, to make them. Despite the distance and time, the flavor of homemade noodles has never lost its magic. "The noodles taste so different from store-bought noodles," says Cathleen. "It's always a hit when we have guests. People are amazed that they're homemade and often say they've never tasted noodles like these before."

Cathleen's homemade noodles are a beautiful reminder that some traditions—whether in Minnesota or Cambodia—are worth carrying on. And that no matter where you are, a bowl of homemade noodles always tastes like home.

SERVES 3–4

2 eggs

1 teaspoon salt

1 tablespoon water

1¼ cups flour, plus more for rolling

In a large bowl, beat eggs, salt, and water. Gradually mix in flour until the dough is very stiff.

On a floured surface, roll out the dough, adding more flour and rubbing it in to get a dry surface on the noodle. Roll as thin as desired and cut noodles with a pizza cutter.

Boil in water or soup for about 4 minutes.

tips Cathleen doesn't always follow the drying method that's traditionally recommended. "In Cambodia, the humidity doesn't really allow for that," she says. "I usually just cut the dough and use it right away."

Cathleen's grandma would say, "Always use one egg for each person eating." Cathleen laughs and adds, "I think that rule was for hardworking farmers. I've never used more than three or four eggs, and it's always enough."

Saltine Cracker Breaded Walleye

Jered Granley
Duluth, MN

the dish

A simple egg wash and crushed crackers are all that's needed to achieve pan-fried walleye perfection.

the tell

My younger brother, Jered, has been fishing ever since he was a toddler, following in the footsteps of many in our family who share a deep passion for the thrill of the catch. Today he estimates spending more than three hundred hours in his boat each summer, not to mention his regular ice fishing escapades on Minnesota's frozen lakes in the winter months. It's safe to say he has caught his fair share of walleye — Minnesota's state fish, much appreciated for its flaky white meat.

When it comes to eating the coveted cuisine, Jered relies on a simple standby recipe handed down from our Grandma Hilma, who loved to fish for walleye with her husband, Joe, on Red Lake near Bemidji, Minnesota. Hilma's walleye breading recipe includes dipping the fillets in an egg wash, rolling them in crushed saltines, and frying in hot oil. "The recipe is so simple, but that's probably why we like it so much," says Jered, who adds it's a convenient meal to pack up and make as a shore lunch when on a fishing trip or for a quick dinner back at the campsite. "You can throw a few sleeves of saltines and some lemons in a gallon-sized bag and then you just need some oil, an egg, and a pan and you have a meal for the whole group."

Assuming, of course, that there has been a successful outing to catch some fish!

SERVES 2–3

1 sleeve saltines

vegetable oil

2 eggs

1 pound walleye

Put the saltines in a large plastic bag and use a coffee mug to crush them into a fine powder.

In a cast iron skillet, heat about a half inch of oil, enough to cover the fillets. While the oil is heating, beat eggs to prepare the egg wash. Test to see if the oil is hot with a splash of egg wash. It will sizzle when ready.

Dip fish into egg wash and shake in cracker mixture. Drop in oil and fry until golden brown, about 2–3 minutes, flipping once if necessary.

tips Cut the fillets into four pieces so they are more like fish sticks.

A little lemon pepper or other seasonings can be added to the batter to give it more flavor.

Jered estimates about one pound of fish per person, but his crew has healthy appetites.

Serve with lemon wedges and tartar sauce.

The recipe works well for frying similar fish like crappies as well as grouse "nuggets," made from chunks of grouse meat.

just for fun

The best advice Jered has picked up from our mom, Carol, and his mother-in-law, Jackie, is to use Sundays to make a nice dinner like roasted meat (see page 70) and to not rush it: "Cook it low and slow."

Dill Butter Carrots

the dish

Buttery, tender carrots with a touch of dill.

the tell

Sometimes the inspiration for a family-favorite recipe comes from a surprising source—which is the case for a tasty side dish that has accompanied our Sunday dinners and made recurring appearances during the holidays and regularly graces my table today.

Dill butter carrots is a recipe I always believed my mom got from a relative like our aunt Ede (the source of so many of our family recipes), an old friend, or a church cookbook. However, I learned my mom got the original recipe from a package of Land O'Lakes butter years ago.

I guess it shouldn't be too surprising. Many of the staple ingredients we find at the grocery store feature recipes on their labels. It's smart marketing, and often these recipes are really quite good. Some, like green bean casserole, which first appeared on a package of French's Crispy Fried Onions, have taken on a life of their own.

While dill butter carrots haven't enjoyed the same path to fame and glory as green bean casserole, they have been an underrated dish that often steals the show at our table. Cooked in butter and dill weed with a little chicken bouillon, the carrots become perfectly tender with a rich flavor that we enjoy alongside everything from Sunday dinners to my mom's Italian shells. Another favorite way to serve these carrots is mixed with leftover rotisserie chicken and rice.

No matter where the recipe originated, it has earned a permanent place at our family table.

SERVES 4–6

4 tablespoons butter

3 cups carrots, peeled and cut into strips

1 teaspoon chicken bouillon

1 teaspoon dried dill

¼ teaspoon salt

fresh dill for garnish, optional

Melt butter in saucepan and stir in carrots, chicken bouillon, dried dill, and salt. Cover and cook over medium heat for 12–15 minutes, until carrots are tender. Garnish with fresh dill if desired.

Creamy Cucumbers

the dish

A light and fresh cucumber side dish with a tangy sour cream dressing.

the tell

Creamy cucumbers, or "Ede's cucumbers" as we call them at my house in honor of my great-aunt, make for a light and refreshing side dish and a good way to use up garden cucumbers when they are in season.

It's a recipe my mom made, but it was her aunt Ede who first introduced it to our family. Ede always had a plentiful garden and was known for making simple yet delicious home-cooked meals. I can imagine Aunt Ede standing in her cozy kitchen that overlooked Cass Lake in northern Minnesota, peeling cucumbers just picked from her garden, and then scoring them with a fork to make them look extra pretty for this dish. She always had that special touch that made for memorable home-cooked meals. Everyone felt lucky to have a seat at her table.

When my mom makes this recipe, she scores the cucumbers with the peel still on before slicing them, which she says adds some nice color to the finished dish. Her advice: Don't apply too much pressure and be sure to use fresh cucumbers or you may end up with a mushy mess.

Another fun twist: I have used a vegetable peeler to peel stripes on the cucumbers before slicing. But honestly, you can simply slice the cucumbers thin without peeling or scoring at all.

Moral of the story? There is more than one way to peel a cucumber! No matter which way you choose, I am sure Aunt Ede would be tickled to know that her recipe for creamy cucumbers lives on and continues to be enjoyed today.

SERVES 3–4

2 cucumbers, sliced thin

2 green onions, chopped

¼ cup vinegar

2 tablespoons sour cream

1½ tablespoons mayonnaise

1 tablespoon sugar

lemon juice

salt

freshly cracked pepper

Place prepared cucumbers and onions in a large bowl. In a small bowl, mix vinegar, sour cream, and mayonnaise. Stir in sugar, lemon juice, salt, and pepper to taste. Add dressing to cucumbers and green onions and toss to coat.

tip Replace sour cream with Top the Tater for some added flavor from the chive and onion seasonings blended in the dip.

What's Cooking?

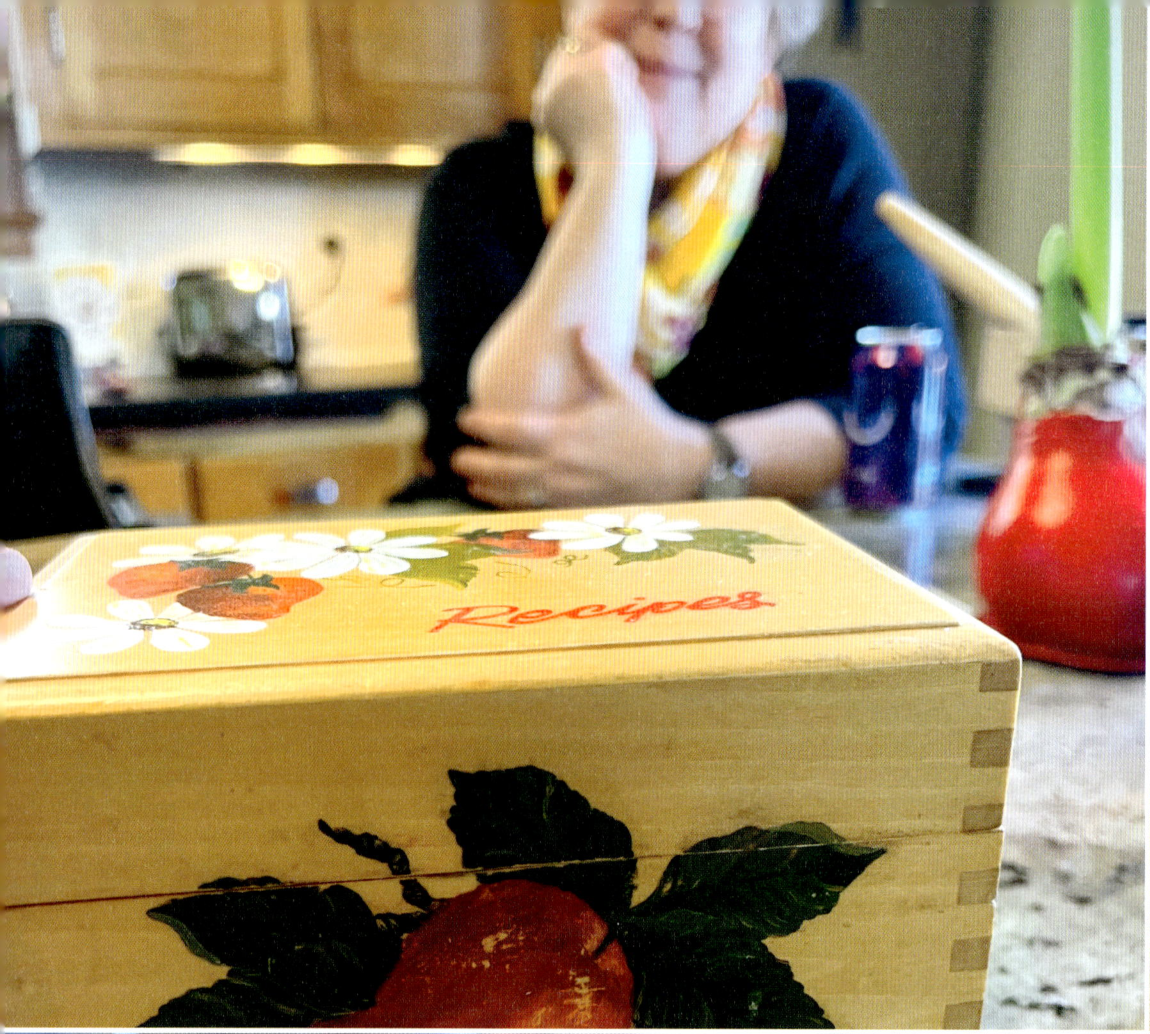

Polly
Here's what's cookin':
Recipe from: mom
1 pound ground beef
5 cups water

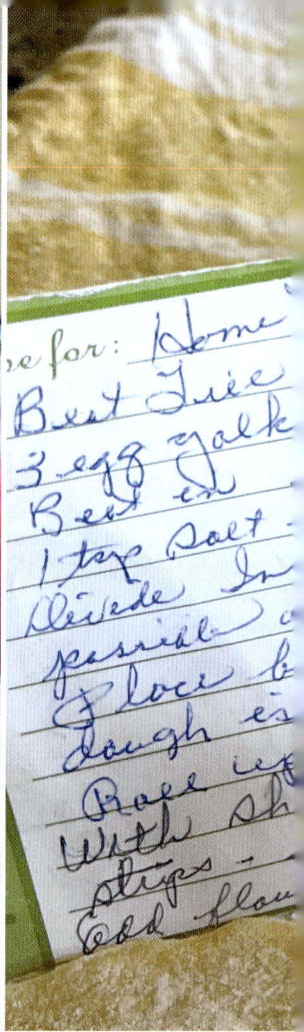

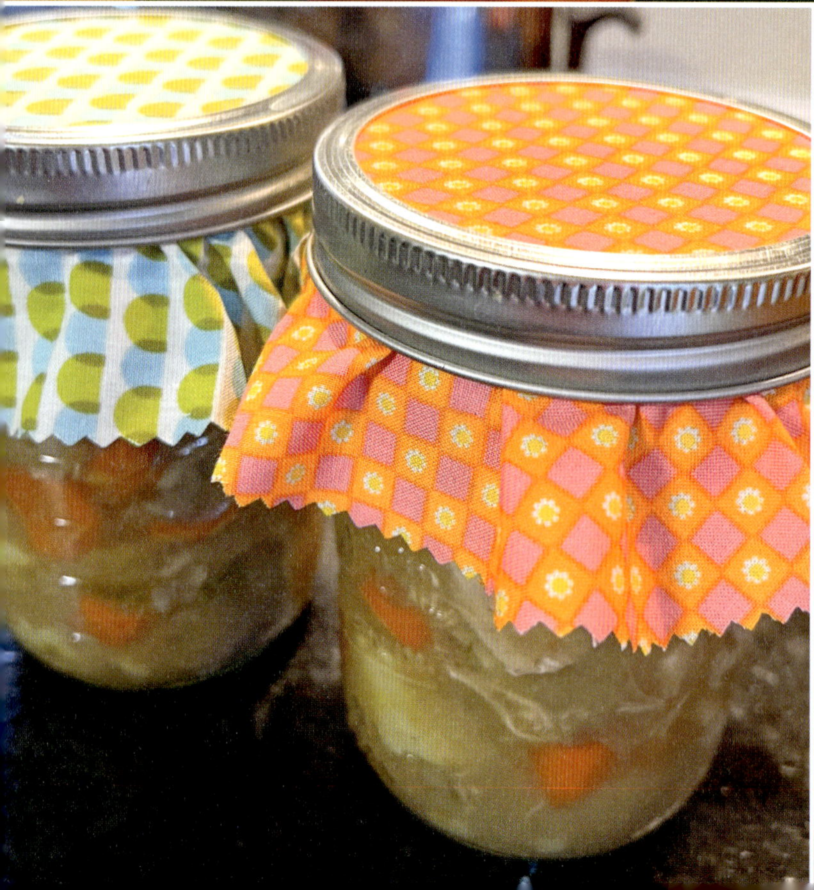

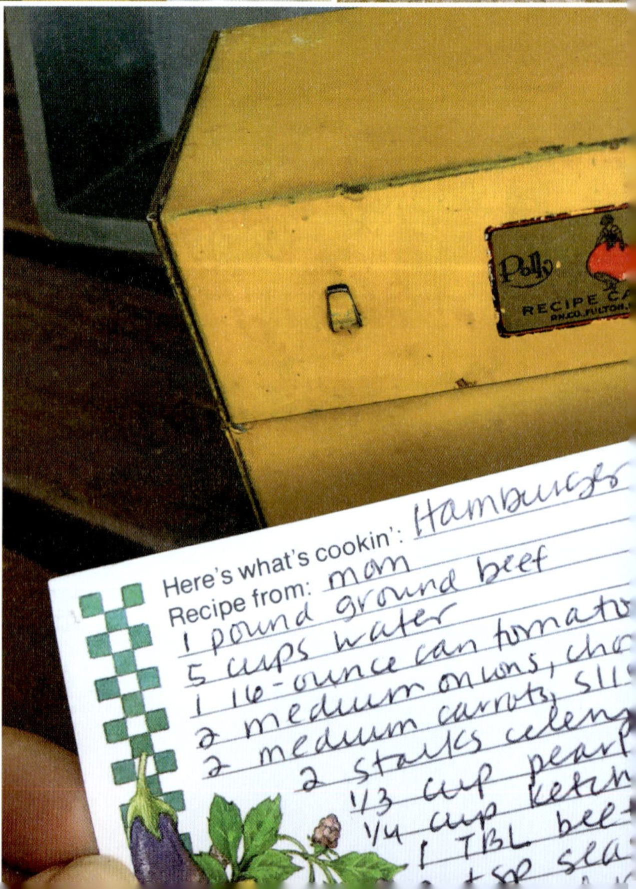

Sentimental Soups & Grandma Bread

Here's what's cookin'

Hamburger Soup 91
Chile Cheese Soup 92
Get Well Chicken Soup with Grandma Ev's Homemade Noodles 94
Kimchi Jjigae 98
Cracked Wheat Bread 101
Grandma Rosamond's Family Bread 104

Homemade soup, synonymous with comfort and care, can be hearty and healing, nostalgic and nourishing. It can even be a meditative journey, from chopping the ingredients to patiently simmering the broth, resulting in a delicious, home-cooked meal. And for many of us, there is one particular soup that will always remind us of home.

For me, hamburger soup checks all the boxes. It's the soup I make when I know my family is craving a hot and tasty meal that is familiar, flavorful, and well loved. Others I spoke with shared similar sentiments about their own family-favorite soups, such as chile cheese soup, "get well" chicken soup with homemade noodles, and kimchi jjigae stew.

And what pairs better with a steaming bowl of homemade soup than some fresh-baked bread?

In conversations about cherished recipes, the discussion often turned to a beloved bread, almost always linked to a grandmother. In my family, that bread was Grandma Hilma's homemade buns. They weren't just a staple at dinner but also a snack between meals. When it came time to leave her house, an ice cream pail full of buns would go with us. I remember being thankful to have easy access to that bucket on our three-hour journey home.

Unfortunately, like many family recipes of yesteryear, my grandmother's buns were made from memory without a written recipe. But some families I spoke with were fortunate to have their versions of "grandma bread" carefully recorded, passing down both the recipes and the techniques to a new generation of bakers.

Beyond traditional loaves and buns, I loved hearing stories of grandmothers and mothers frying bread dough and transforming it into irresistible treats. In addition to Jami Vandenberg's story about her grandmother's flutchies (see page 35), others shared how these simple delights carried deep memories.

Becky Brandt, who researched her family's food traditions for a family cookbook, learned her great-grandma Lena made what she called "flutchens" or "fry bread." While she never got to try Lena's specialty, her mom and grandma had fond memories of the bread that was deep-fried and dusted with powdered sugar, granulated sugar, or honey.

Shannon Thomasser reminisced: "My mom would make homemade bread dough and fry it. We called them 'dough gods,' and they were delicious! We would put butter and homemade maple syrup on them and eat and eat and eat. She would just keep frying and we would keep eating!"

Jeanie Thomas's family had a similar treat, but they called them dough dogs. Rather than waste leftover dough, they cut it into the size of a chicken nugget, fried it until golden brown, and topped it with syrup, turning scraps into something unforgettable.

Whether it's a simmering pot of soup or a warm, buttery piece of fresh-baked bread or fried dough, these recipes hold the flavors of our childhoods and memories of those who made them with love.

Hamburger Soup

the dish

A tasty and hearty broth-based soup featuring ground beef, crushed tomatoes, pearl barley, and a variety of vegetables.

the tell

Even though this soup has been a part of my life since childhood, it wasn't until I was an adult that I came to love it. I now fully appreciate its simplicity, and it has become one of my go-to meals when my own family craves some cozy comfort food.

The original recipe was printed in my hometown newspaper back in the eighties. Like many of my mom's most treasured recipes, the clipping is taped to an index card and tucked into her collection of family favorites that reside in a small Rubbermaid container. The recipe was simply credited to someone with the initials C.D. It's a shame we don't know who the contributor was to thank them for this wonderful soup that has been a staple in our family for years.

When my dad's health was declining and he was in his last week, his appetite was changing, and I made a batch of soup to share with him. Since my mom has been making it for years, I knew it would be a familiar dish to my dad and was relieved he was able to eat and maybe even enjoy it just a little. It was one of the last meals we had together.

Later that same week, this soup reemerged when our family needed it most. In those first blurred days of grief, our longtime neighbor Sharon—who has exchanged countless recipes with our family over the years—delivered a fresh batch of hamburger soup, complete with crackers and fresh bread. We acknowledged the coincidence that we both turned to the same comforting recipe during a difficult time. It was a touching reminder that a family recipe made with love can bring comfort and a sense of home in a way nothing else can.

SERVES 8–10

1 pound ground beef

butter

5 cups water

1 (14.5-ounce) can diced tomatoes

2 medium onions, chopped (about 1 cup)

2 medium carrots, sliced (about 1 cup)

2 ribs celery, sliced (about 1 cup)

⅓ cup pearl barley (see tip)

¼ cup ketchup

1 tablespoon beef bouillon

1 teaspoon seasoned salt

1 teaspoon dried basil

1 bay leaf

salt and pepper

In a Dutch oven or stockpot set over medium heat, brown ground beef in a little butter. Drain excess fat. Add water, tomatoes, onions, carrots, celery, barley, ketchup, beef bouillon, seasoned salt, basil, and bay leaf. Bring to a boil, reduce heat, and simmer, covered, for 1 hour or until vegetables are tender. Remove bay leaf and season with salt and pepper to taste.

tips To make this soup gluten-free, replace the pearl barley with brown or white rice. Cook the rice separately, adding it to the soup at the last moment so the rice doesn't get mushy.

My favorite way to eat this soup is with a side of Cheeze-Its.

Jeanie Thomas
Eden Prairie, MN

Linda Thomas
Moorhead, MN

Chile Cheese Soup

the dish

A comforting, flavorful cheese soup with chopped carrots, celery, and green chiles.

the tell

Spending an afternoon with Jeanie and her mom, Linda, reminded me just how perfectly fresh-baked bread pairs with a warm bowl of soup. Though we initially set out to bake their family's Grandma Bread—featured on page 101—my gracious hosts insisted I try it the way they frequently enjoy it: paired with another longtime family-favorite recipe, chile cheese soup.

The delicious, creamy concoction is not your typical Midwestern cheese soup. The inclusion of green chiles and a dash of paprika adds a subtle, smoky heat. It's such a flavorful, enticing soup that people have been known to go to extremes to get it. Linda recalled a funny story: One time when she made the soup, her granddaughter Morgan, who lives nearby, got so excited she leaped over the fence and into her grandma's kitchen to get her share!

While Linda first introduced the recipe to the family, it has since become a staple in Jeanie's home as well. She prepares it often in the fall during football season, serving it with homemade bread or tortilla chips. For Jeanie, her wife Larissa, and their daughters, this dish is a cherished connection to Grandma Linda, who has frequently made it during visits to their home in Eden Prairie throughout the years.

Jeanie also appreciates the soup's versatility: It can be made gluten-free with gluten-free flour or vegetarian with vegetable broth or turned into a heartier soup with the addition of shredded chicken. No matter how it's served, it remains a reminder of family, tradition, and the simple joy of homemade food.

tips **Try different cheeses such as a Mexican cheese blend.**

If adding chicken, Jeanie suggests cutting up half of a store-bought rotisserie chicken or, even better, roasting your own to make a "killer broth."

The soup can be frozen: Hold the dairy and add it later, when ready to heat and serve.

just for fun In addition to her fabulous mom, Jeanie credits Grandma Bing and Aunt Nancy for their influence on her special food memories and her family's food traditions. She says Aunt Nancy, who made everything from scratch, was a big inspiration to her in the kitchen. One of her favorite memories is how Nancy would eat krumkake: stuffed with homemade whipped cream!

Grandma Bing, who was known for her delicious homemade pies, always kept an extra crust or two at the ready in her freezer for when fruit was in season or when company was coming to town. She would make a large batch of crusts with a recipe using 7UP as a key ingredient and then freeze the crusts in separate portions.

SERVES 6–8

½ cup (1 stick) butter

½ onion, grated

2 carrots, grated

2 ribs celery, chopped

2 tablespoons flour

sprinkle paprika

2 (14.5-ounce) cans chicken or vegetable broth

1 pint half-and-half or heavy cream

2 (4-ounce) cans chopped chiles

8 ounces shredded cheddar cheese

chopped or shredded cooked chicken, optional

In a Dutch oven or stockpot, melt butter and cook onions, carrots, and celery for about 5–10 minutes, stirring often, until vegetables are tender. Stir in flour and a sprinkle of paprika. Gradually stir in broth and dairy. Bring to a boil and cook until thickened, stirring frequently. Reduce heat and add chiles and cheese, stirring until cheese is melted. Add chicken (if using).

Get Well Chicken Soup with Grandma Ev's Homemade Noodles

Carol Wilkie
St. Paul, MN

the dish

A perfect pick-me-up chicken soup full of flavor and love.

the tell

My sweet neighbor Carol described an "aha moment" she had after the birth of her first child when she experienced firsthand the impact of a home-cooked meal—how it can be nourishing, comforting, and uplifting. "My mom and sister drove up from Iowa to celebrate the occasion, and they carried in a big batch of this soup," says Carol. "I still remember how wonderful it tasted—and how much I needed that special care."

Now the chicken soup is Carol's go-to recipe for friends and family who are sick, are welcoming a new baby, or simply need extra love and warmth. Food has always been Carol's way of expressing care. She recalls that after her grandmother passed away when she was five, it became a family ritual to prepare meals for her grandpa. Her mom would pack a plate from their nightly dinner, and they'd deliver it to his farm, ensuring he always had home-cooked meals.

Today Carol continues the tradition of providing nourishing meals for loved ones—most often through her signature chicken soup. She has slightly modified the recipe through the years, adding her own special touch, including homemade noodles. She notes that the recipe is not a rush-through project but one she enjoys stretching out over two days. "I find it a grounding, meditative process," she says.

On day one Carol makes the stock: It's a great way to use up veggie scraps from the kitchen. On day two she rolls up her sleeves to make the homemade pasta, using a treasured egg noodle recipe passed down from her elderly neighbor, Evelyn.

Grandma Ev, as Carol and her family affectionately called her, was the kind of special neighbor you could rely on, whether it was for a cup of sugar or to watch the kids in a pinch. Ev had spent her life cooking for others, including the famous advice columnist Ann Landers, who once lived in the high-rise apartment building where Evelyn worked. As Evelyn aged, Carol's family eventually started plating food from their nightly dinners for her—just as Carol's mom had done for her grandpa decades earlier.

Carol packages this soup in pint jars to deliver to loved ones or have on hand for her family. The jars can even be frozen for later use—but chances are no one will wait that long to enjoy this comforting dish. »

Get Well Chicken Soup with Grandma Ev's Homemade Noodles

MAKES 6–8 PINTS

soup

1 pound carrots, peeled and cut into half-inch pieces (save the ends and peels for stock)

1 package celery, cut into half-inch pieces (cut off ends and leafy greens to save for stock)

2 yellow onions, chopped (save peel and ends for stock)

8 bone-in, skin-on chicken thighs

1 bunch thyme, divided

3 bay leaves

1 teaspoon cumin

1 teaspoon salt

1 teaspoon pepper

homemade egg noodles (recipe follows)

1 (14-ounce) carton chicken broth, optional

heavy cream, optional

noodles

2 cups flour

1 whole egg plus 3 egg yolks

1 teaspoon salt

3 tablespoons cold water

Day one: Prepare the veggies and make stock.

Prep the vegetables for the soup while simultaneously setting aside the scraps—peelings, ends, leafy greens—for stock. Set aside the prepped vegetables in a resealable container.

Place the vegetable scraps (not the chopped vegetables themselves) in a large stockpot. Place the chicken thighs on top and then add half the thyme and the bay leaves, cumin, salt, and pepper. Fill the stockpot with warm water, to about 2 inches from the top of the pan. Cover the pot, bring the stock to a boil, then reduce heat and simmer for 3 hours. Cook the stock gently so the chicken doesn't become tough.

Next, remove chicken pieces and let them cool (the remaining stock can continue to simmer on the stove). When the chicken has cooled slightly, remove the meat from the bones, gently pulling the pieces into bite-size morsels. Return the bones, fat, and skin to the stockpot. Package and refrigerate the chicken pieces.

Continue to simmer the stock for 1 hour. Turn off the heat, allow to cool, and then put the entire pot of stock into the refrigerator.

Day two: Drain the stock; make noodles; make and package soup.

Remove the chilled pot of stock/veggies from the refrigerator. Skim off the fat layer that has risen to the top. A little of this fat is fine, as it will add some flavor to the soup, but you don't want a lot.

Heat the soup just enough so that it loses its gelatinous state. Remove the larger pieces of bone and vegetables with a slotted spoon. Set a fine strainer in a bowl and drain the rest of the stock through the strainer. Discard all solids and return stock to the original pot.

To make the noodles, place the flour in a medium bowl.

In a separate dish, use a fork to lightly beat egg yolks and whole egg. Add salt and cold water and beat with a fork until salt dissolves. Add egg mixture to flour and stir.

Work the dough gently until all flour is incorporated. The mixture will be crumbly at first but should begin to form into a smooth dough as you gently work it. Resist the urge to add more water. Form the dough into a ball, cover with a towel, and let rest for 20 minutes.

Divide dough into 3 equal parts. Working on a floured surface, roll each portion as thinly as possible. (A pasta machine works great for this step, but you can also use a rolling pin.) If you like strip noodles, roll up the dough like a jelly roll and cut noodles at the desired width. Unroll and cover with a towel until ready to use. If you like square homestyle noodles, place the rolled dough on a floured towel and cut into squares using a scalloped pastry cutter, knife, or pizza cutter.

Soup time!

Bring the strained stock to a boil. If you want more liquid, add a carton of store-bought chicken stock. Add the remaining thyme, stems and all, and boil for about 5 minutes, or until the thyme leaves fall off the stems. Remove thyme stems with a slotted spoon and discard.

Reduce heat to medium. Add chopped carrots, celery, and onions, and cook in the broth until tender, about 20 minutes. Add noodles and cook for another 10–15 minutes.

Reduce heat to low. Add the reserved chicken meat and cook until heated through. Season with salt and pepper as needed.

If serving immediately, add a splash of heavy cream for a creamy version.

To package for loved ones

After the soup has simmered and the flavors have been incorporated, fill pint jars with hot soup, leaving ¾ inch at the top, and cover immediately. Cool on the counter until the lids seal.

Soup can be stored in the refrigerator for 3–4 days or can be frozen.

tips **Anything is game as you make the stock! Carrot peels and ends, the root and leafy parts of celery, onion skins, and anything else in your refrigerator that needs to be recycled. Carol sometimes drops in a couple of small onions (whole, peels and all) if they seem like they're getting a little soft in her root cellar.**

Carol suggests keeping a bread bag in your freezer for veggie scraps that can be used in the stock when you're ready to make soup.

To cool the stock in winter, Carol puts the pot outside. However, she advises that you should "make sure the cover is secure, and it is placed up on a table so no critters can investigate."

When straining the stock, don't forget to put a large bowl underneath the colander. Carol once strained a whole batch of stock into the sink in a moment she calls "utter brainlessness!"

When making homemade noodles, fill a sifter with flour for an easy way to add flour where necessary. Don't worry about the extra flour on the noodles; it will help thicken the soup.

When cleaning up floured surfaces, bowls, or even your hands, use cold water, not hot, and soap. Carol says, "That way, the flour won't gum up on you."

just for fun About the packaged soup, Carol says, "For an extra perky treat, you can place a fabric cover on top of the jars."

Carol has the cutest recipe box, hand-painted by her mom and filled with many handwritten recipes.

Carol has a great hack for a tasty pie crust she learned from her mom: Add a teaspoon of lemon juice.

Kimchi Jjigae

Kim Jackson
Minnetonka, MN

the dish

A tasty and hearty version of the traditional Korean stew, customized with the addition of noodles and rice cakes—or not—to suit individual preferences.

the tell

My friend Kim's recipe for kimchi jjigae, a popular Korean stew, is one she has honed with her own special "Kim twists," to the delight of her family and friends who frequently request this nourishing dish of comfort-in-a-bowl.

The stew gets its tangy flavor from kimchi (fermented cabbage) and a touch of spiciness from ingredients like gochujang (red chili paste) and gochucharu (red chili flakes). Other traditional components of jjigae include ingredients such as tofu, pork belly, sliced peppers, and mushrooms.

Kim's version layers in potato starch noodles, rice cakes, and scrambled egg, which all add heartiness and "heart." These ingredients are the final touches Kim happily adapts on the fly to give her husband and kids their own custom jjigae bowl to suit their tastes. "The beauty of this stew is that you can customize it so it's unique to the person eating it," says Kim. "People often make it their own."

For Kim, jjigae isn't just a stew: It represents her ongoing journey to learn about Korean culture and foods. Growing up in Minnesota after being adopted from Korea in 1975 when she was almost four years old, Kim didn't have exposure to Korean food or recipes as a child. When her mom cooked, the meals ranged from hotdish to fried chicken. "There was very little spice," says Kim, who adds that her mom had a few Korean recipes but likely found them too challenging to make because access to certain ingredients was limited back then.

Later in life Kim had the opportunity to travel to and from Korea, and she developed a taste for Korean foods and a palate for increasing levels of spice. On her first trip, just after high school graduation, Kim recalls a pivotal food memory with a particular soup. It was the first time she ever had yukgaejang, a spicy beef soup with vegetables and noodles that she recalls, "was blaring spicy but so good." It quickly became her favorite food in Korea and ignited her passion for Korean cuisine.

Through several trips back to Korea and her involvement with the Korean community in Minnesota, Kim's love for Korean food expanded, and she continued to develop her cooking skills. Soon she was making more of her favorite dishes like jjigae at home.

Today, kimchi jjigae is a dish Kim makes all year round, whether for a special occasion or simply to use up leftover kimchi, which is often the case thanks to Kim's close friend Kara, who happens to be my sister-in-law. Kara prefers kimchi when it's fresh; once it starts to get a bit too sour she brings her leftovers straight to Kim to instigate a jjigae get-together. Kim jokes that Kara is her supplier but admits it's good to dine with friends who enjoy jjigae.

Kim's recipe makes a big pot of jjigae, perfect for sharing. She serves it as a main course complete with banchans—a variety of side dishes such as fresh kimchi, bean sprouts, cooked spinach, and rice. These items are all served in little dishes and can be eaten as a side or, as Kim notes, can be added to the main dish "to make it your own bowl."

Thanks to Kim's efforts to revisit her roots and hone her cooking skills, she is passing her love for Korean cuisine to her kids, who she is proud to say are adventurous eaters with a tolerance for spice. Jjigae is one of several Korean dishes she has brought to the table to share with her family and friends, ensuring important traditions will live on for generations to come.

Kimchi Jjigae

SERVES 4–6

1½ –2 cups leftover kimchi (enough to fill one-third of a large saucepan)

1 cup chicken broth

1 tablespoon gochujang (red chili paste)

1 tablespoon gochucharu (Korean red chili flakes)

1½ teaspoons soy sauce

1½ teaspoons sesame oil

1 teaspoon sugar or honey, to taste

2 cloves garlic, chopped or minced

salt and pepper to taste

garlic salt to taste, optional

1 (12-ounce) package firm tofu, cut into 10–12 bite-size cubes

½ cup dried shiitake mushrooms

1–2 eggs, beaten

2 green onions, chopped into 2-inch pieces

handful potato starch noodles

1½ cups Korean rice cakes

for serving: rice and banchan such as fresh kimchi, bean sprouts, cooked spinach

Combine kimchi, broth, gochujang, gochucharu, soy sauce, sesame oil, sugar, garlic, salt, pepper, and garlic salt (if using) in a large jjigae pot or saucepan. Add water to fill the pot to about half an inch from the rim. Bring to a boil, then simmer for 45 minutes, adding water as needed to maintain the same level of stew.

Add tofu and mushrooms. Return stew to a slight boil, then add egg(s) and let scramble for about 2 minutes. Add green onions and noodles and cook until the noodles soften, about 5 minutes. Add rice cakes and cook for just 2 minutes (and no longer or you risk mushy rice cakes).

Serve with rice and banchan.

tips This recipe is a great way to use "less fresh" kimchi for a more tangy flavor in the stew.

Kimchi is readily available at many grocers, but Kim prefers to buy it in bulk at Costco or an Asian grocer.

Kim, who admittedly nerds out on noodles, says thinner noodles like cellophane noodles are best for this stew. The potato starch noodles she uses for her jjigae recipe are the same ones used in another family-favorite Korean dish called japchae.

just for fun Kim's most sentimental item in her kitchen is the big red Betty Crocker spoon that belonged to her mother-in-law, Jane. "I love how it reminds me of both her and my mom, who had a Betty Crocker cookbook."

She credits her husband, Tom, for being her biggest influencer when it comes to cooking: "Since marrying him, I have cooked or have tried to cook more in the past several years than in my entire adult years."

Kim has a fun hack for making homemade noodles. When it comes time to knead the dough, she uses her feet! She explains, "I have a hard time kneading bread by hand due to no upper body strength and a trick elbow from a past gymnastics accident, so I put the dough into a quart-size plastic bag, then in a large paper bag and start stomping and dancing on the paper bag." She takes out the dough and folds it a couple of times, repeating the paper bag dancing technique for approximately four to five rounds. It makes the kneading process much easier for her. Side note: Kim adds that she later witnessed older Korean women using a similar method to make cold noodle stews in a Korean documentary—which only validates that Kim had this technique in her DNA all along.

Cracked Wheat Bread

Linda Thomas
Moorhead, MN

the dish

Cracked wheat bread has a slightly nutty flavor with an irresistible texture thanks to a grandma's special touch and techniques honed over time.

the tell

If there's a bread that appeals to all the senses, it is this cracked wheat bread. From the handling of the dough to the smell of the bread baking in the oven to the grand finale, turning out warm, golden loaves ready to slather with butter—this bread is everything!

I had the opportunity to experience it all when I joined my friend Jeanie and her mom, Linda, to bake the bread their family lovingly coined "Grandma Bread." Jeanie explains that when her mom visits, she often shows up with four or five loaves of bread—one ready to eat and the rest packaged to freeze for later. "Our kids have fond memories of this bread and expect it when grandma visits, hence the name," says Jeanie.

It's a recipe Linda has been baking for more than twenty years, ever since she got it from her sister-in-law Margie, who worked for the North Dakota Wheat Commission. It was part of a collection the commission shared to promote the use of wheat products. "I started making the bread after eating it at her house and watching her make it," says Linda, who was raising her family on a farm outside of rural Moorhead, Minnesota. Over the years she has baked it hundreds of times, refining the process with her preferred ingredients and techniques to achieve the best results.

One key difference from other homemade breads is that this recipe calls for cracked wheat, which is coarsely ground from wheat berries and enhances the texture of baked goods with a slight crunchiness. Linda buys it in bulk and stores it in the freezer so she's always ready to bake bread, which she estimates is about every two weeks.

Beyond making Grandma Bread for everyday use, Linda likes to have it on hand for family visits since everyone enjoys it. She recalls a few times when her youngest grandchild, Hudson, wasn't interested in what was being served at mealtime. No problem: Grandma Bread to the rescue!

While Hudson enjoys his slices toasted with butter and grape jelly, Linda prefers hers toasted and topped with butter, most often at breakfast. Occasionally she'll add honey or jelly. She also likes to have this bread on hand for sandwiches and saves the ends to make breadcrumbs for meatballs. Jeanie loves that the bread is sturdy enough for a sandwich yet perfectly tasty with a simple slathering of butter. "Kids who are white bread eaters don't find it scary, and whole wheat bread people like the cracked wheat in it," says Jeanie. "Everyone loves Grandma Bread."

It's probably no surprise that Linda, an amazing home cook and baker, has several other specialties she makes at the request of Jeanie and her sister, their spouses, and her four grandchildren. From lefse and apple bars to chile cheese soup (see page 92)—and, of course, her much-loved bread—Linda exemplifies what it means to cook from the heart for those she loves. "Part of what makes this bread so special is that she is the one who bakes it," says Jeanie. ➤➤

Cracked Wheat Bread

for 2 loaves (6-quart bowl)

3 cups boiling water

1½ cups cracked wheat

2 (¼-ounce) packets active dry yeast

½ cup warm water (110–115 degrees)

¼ cup oil

¼ cup honey

6–7 cups bread flour

2 teaspoons salt

for 1 loaf (4-quart bowl)

1½ cups boiling water

¾ cup cracked wheat

1 (¼-ounce) packet active dry yeast

¼ cup warm water (110–115 degrees)

2 tablespoons oil

2 tablespoons honey

3–3½ cups bread flour

1 teaspoon salt

In the large bowl of a stand mixer, stir together boiling water and cracked wheat. Cool to 110 degrees, about 15 to 20 minutes.

Dissolve yeast in warm water. Grease a large bowl and 1 or 2 (9x5–inch) pans; set aside.

To cracked wheat mixture, add oil, honey, yeast mixture, and 1 cup flour if making one loaf or 2 cups if making two loaves. Beat on low speed using paddle attachment until blended. Increase speed and beat 2 minutes, until smooth. Add salt and mix thoroughly. Swap out the paddle attachment for a dough hook and add 2 cups flour (for one loaf) or 4 cups flour (for two loaves). Knead for approximately 12 minutes, adding additional flour as needed, until dough is smooth and elastic.

Place in greased bowl, turning dough to coat top. Cover with plastic wrap. Let rise in a warm place 1–1½ hours or until doubled in size.

Punch down, form into 1 or 2 loaves, and place in prepared pan(s). Let rise about 1 hour, until doubled. Heat oven to 450 degrees.

Bake for 10 minutes, then reduce temperature to 350 degrees and bake 30–35 minutes, until loaf sounds hollow when tapped with fingers. Tent with foil during last 15 minutes to prevent overbrowning. Remove from pan to cooling rack.

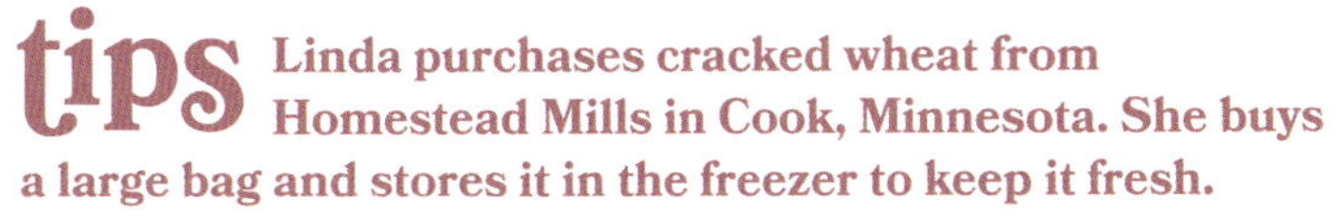

tips Linda purchases cracked wheat from Homestead Mills in Cook, Minnesota. She buys a large bag and stores it in the freezer to keep it fresh.

She buys yeast in bulk from Costco and stores it in the refrigerator or freezer to extend its shelf life.

When activating the yeast, stir into warm water and add a little sugar; when the mixture bubbles you'll know it's not out of date.

When greasing the pans, Linda prefers Crisco since it contains no salt, which can affect the dough's texture.

just for fun Some of Linda's most cherished kitchen items include her mom's Pyrex bread bowl as well as a crockery bread bowl that she bought shortly after her aunt taught her how to bake bread.

Grandma Rosamond's Family Bread

Jeanie Cheeley
Dayton, MN

the dish

A delightfully dark bread made with rolled oats and molasses, hand-kneaded with love (and optional dough tossing) that makes it as fun to make as it is to eat.

the tell

Jeanie, mom to my friend Kara, has a recipe for oatmeal bread that she makes often—both for the nostalgia that ties the recipe to her mother and for new memories created from making the bread with her grandchildren. It's a delicious bread that is not overly complicated to make. No mixer or dough hook is required: It's best when kneaded gently by hand to achieve a tender dark bread with a subtle sweetness.

Jeanie's mother, Rosamond, got the recipe from a church cookbook titled *Favorite Recipes of Diamond Lake Church*. It's a plentiful source of "tested recipes" from the ladies' guild associated with the Minneapolis church. Rosamond referred to the cookbook frequently when she cooked and baked for her family, and Jeanie still uses it to this day.

The oatmeal bread became a favorite recipe among Jeanie's family while she was growing up. Even though making bread was a time-consuming process, Jeanie says that many people in her mom's generation did so regularly. It was a different day and age. "Women were 'homemakers,' wore housedresses, and stayed home all day," says Jeanie. "While the bread was rising, they might be washing clothes in a wringer machine and hanging them outside to dry on the clothesline."

Some of the other family-favorite dishes from Rosamond's recipe collection that Jeanie and her family still enjoy include rhubarb Bundt cake, carrot cake, Swedish meatballs, fruit salad, lasagna casserole, and gingersnaps.

Today Jeanie keeps a clipping of the original oatmeal bread recipe on an index card with notes from her grandchildren, who thought it deserved a more meaningful name: Grandma Rosamond's Family Bread. She cherishes the moments when all four of her grandkids are present and they've baked the family bread together. Kate and Kindra, cousins around the same age and automatic best friends, have made making this bread a tradition along with their respective brothers, Sam and Grey, pitching in from time to time. Once when they were all making the bread together, the kids got excited about the big ball of dough and said, "Let's play catch!" Jeanie says they all went into hysterics as they threw the ball back and forth to each other, and a new tradition was born.

MAKES 2 LOAVES

1 (¼-ounce) packet active dry yeast

½ cup warm water (110–115 degrees)

¼ cup plus 1 teaspoon sugar, divided

1 cup rolled oats

2 cups water

2 tablespoons butter

1 teaspoon salt

¼ cup molasses

5 cups all-purpose or bread flour

In a small bowl, stir together yeast, ½ cup warm water, and 1 teaspoon sugar. Let stand for 10–15 minutes until the yeast is activated. Grease a large bowl and 2 (9x5–inch) loaf pans; set aside.

To a saucepan set over medium heat, add oats and 2 cups water and bring to a boil; remove from heat and stir in butter, salt, molasses, and remaining ¼ cup sugar. Transfer mixture to a mixing bowl and let cool for approximately 20 minutes.

Add the yeast mixture and flour; stir to combine.

Knead the dough by hand on a floured surface until smooth and elastic. Let rise in greased bowl until doubled in size, about 3 hours. Divide into 2 loaves and place in prepared pans. Let rise again until doubled or just above the rim of the pan. Heat oven to 375 degrees. Bake for 45 minutes (see Sarah's notes).

just for fun

Jeanie's grandkids Kindra and Grey in their younger years often made little pigs out of the dough—another fun way to "knead" this bread!

Sarah's notes

Before baking, brush some egg white beaten with water on top of the loaf and sprinkle with rolled oats.

If the bread starts to brown too quickly, tent with aluminum foil for the final portion of baking.

tips

Jeanie uses butter but says her mom used lard as called for in the original recipe.

The amount of flour needed may vary slightly depending on the dough's texture. Jeanie says it shouldn't stick to the counter when kneading, but it shouldn't be too dry.

The best texture comes from hand-kneading, but Jeanie says it's up to you if you want to toss the dough around the room to your loved ones.

After a few days, Jeanie likes to use the bread to make toast. "It's very good with butter and honey."

Like all homemade breads with no preservatives, these loaves don't keep for long; however, this probably won't be a problem since it's so good you'll want to eat it right away.

Potlucks & Party Food

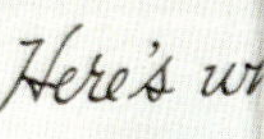

Here's what's cookin'

Ede's (Kid-Friendly) Slush
aka Tropical Banana Slush 109
Rhubarb Slush 110
Buffalo Chicken Dip 112
Sue's Dip 114
Salami Chips 115
BLT Bites 117
Sandwich Loaf 118
Layered Tortellini Salad 123
Dill Pickle Pasta Salad 124
Crunchy Coleslaw 126

Potlucks are where recipes from the heart come to shine. These informal get-togethers where everyone brings "a little something to share" represent Hall of Fame comfort food that everyone loves to eat and dishes that are often the cherished family recipes people are most proud of and eager to talk about.

One of my first grown-up experiences with potlucks, when I was asked to contribute a dish, was when I worked at the University of Minnesota as a student secretary in the Department of Psychiatry. I don't remember much about my official job duties, but I had a wonderful supervisor named Kelly, a fellow northern Minnesota gal who was more of a "partner in crime" than a boss. Let's just say there were lots of laughs and leisurely lunches that turned us into lifetime friends.

One of our tasks was coordinating the occasional office potluck where there was always an array of unique dishes thanks to the diverse group of people, which included medical students, professors, and staff of all ages and from many walks of life, not to mention different corners of the world. It was a thrill to see what everyone would bring, from the disheveled grad student who'd show up with a bag of chips to the professor who introduced me to my first bite of tabouli with pita bread—oh my!

Fast-forward to years later: My in-laws regularly hosted a Fourth of July party at their home on Lake Sarah near Independence, Minnesota. They'd fire up the grill for hot dogs and hamburgers, and the fifty or so guests were invited to bring a dish to share. There were no assignments, but like magic we'd end up with the perfect assortment of appetizers, sides, salads, and desserts. I always appreciated the "salad" table for the variety of pasta salads and dishes like fluff, glorified rice, or Snickers salad that leaned a little closer to dessert. Many of my favorites, like self-filled cupcakes, salami chips, creamy cucumbers, and BLT bites, have made their way into this book.

More recently my potluck experience revolved around my daughter's college swim team at Gustavus Adolphus in St. Peter, Minnesota. These were potlucks of epic proportion, feeding more than eighty swimmers and their fan base of family members and friends following home meets. My husband, Jaye, and I had the pleasure of helping to facilitate these feasts, from the sign-up of meals to the controlled chaos of setup.

Meet Days were always a whirlwind with so much action in and out of the pool. Parents would arrive toting coolers and/or armed with slow cookers (SO many slow cookers) to set up before the meet. As the swim meets stretched into hours-long events, parents would tend to their slow cookers, visiting their "special" dish multiple times for a stir or temperature check. It was a treat to see the variety of dishes that leaned on the heartier side—Buffalo chicken dip, sloppy joes, shredded pork, ginormous pasta salads—knowing we were feeding ravenous swimmers as well as family members who had tirelessly cheered them on for hours on end.

No matter the occasion, potlucks have a unique way of bringing people together through treasured dishes that often reflect the heart and soul of the cook behind them. There's something special about seeing a table filled with tried-and-true dishes that have been passed down through generations or perfected over the years and seeing people light up when they talk about their family-favorite dish.

Ede's (Kid-Friendly) Slush aka Tropical Banana Slush

Eric Schmidt
Bemidji, MN

the dish

A tropical-flavored, kid-friendly slush that's as perfect for a punch bowl at a party as it is for an ice cream bucket that sits in the freezer, ready for hot summer days.

the tell

My cousin Eric and I share more than DNA: We share a deep love and admiration for our great-aunt Ede. In addition to being a fabulous cook and baker, Ede was a passionate gardener and had a knack for creating a cozy, inviting home. Above all, she was the ultimate hostess: Whether bringing together a large group for a home-cooked meal or inviting a friend or loved one over for impromptu coffee, she made every encounter seem effortless yet memorable.

Eric was lucky to grow up in the same neighborhood as Ede and got to visit her and our uncle Johnnie regularly. A former teacher, Ede was very fond of kids, and when Eric and his sister Heidi visited she served them cookies or other treats like slush that she kept at the ready in an ice cream bucket in her freezer. Ede's recipe card simply refers to the delicious drink as "slush," but it's a tropical-flavored medley of pineapple and orange juices, lemonade, and whipped bananas topped with lemon-lime soda or ginger ale.

Eric loved that Ede would serve him and his sister the slush in vintage milk glass tumblers with a honeycomb-patterned base, which she later gifted to him along with the beloved recipe. He still can't believe Ede trusted them with the fancy glasses when they were kids, but it made the slush all the more memorable. "It didn't matter that I was just a clumsy kid," says Eric. "This was just one example of how Ede always went out of her way to make us feel welcome and special."

SERVES 40

3 cups sugar

6 cups water

5 bananas

1 (46-ounce) can unsweetened pineapple juice

1 (12-ounce) can frozen orange juice concentrate

1 (6-ounce) can frozen lemonade

lemon-lime soda or ginger ale

Make a simple syrup by adding sugar and water to a saucepan and bringing just to a boil. Stir to dissolve sugar, then set aside to cool completely.

Whip bananas in a blender until smooth. Transfer to a large mixing bowl, pour in pineapple juice, and set aside. Using a blender, blend frozen orange juice concentrate and frozen lemonade with simple syrup. Add to mixing bowl with banana-pineapple mixture and stir to mix. Pour into gallon freezer bags or an ice cream bucket and freeze several hours.

When ready to serve, scoop some slush into a cup and top with an equal amount of lemon-lime soda or ginger ale.

Punch bowl variation: Freeze the slush in a Bundt pan or Jell-O mold. When ready to serve, gently transfer slush to a punch bowl and pour soda on top. Garnish with pineapple rings and cherries.

Rhubarb Slush

the dish

A refreshingly sweet and tart summer sipper made with rhubarb.

the tell

Every late spring, as my backyard rhubarb struggles to keep up with my ambitious plans, I need to call in some reinforcements so I can check off all the items on my rhubarb bucket list—jam, bars, pie, and more. One friend, Doreen, has been generous through the years, sharing from her bounty of beautiful rhubarb growing in the backyard of her home in Cloquet, Minnesota. Her rhubarb is *huge*: It must be that rich Up North soil! Thanks to her kindness, I always have more than enough to make all my rhubarb dreams come true.

Among my favorite ways to use this tart and vibrant ingredient is rhubarb slush—a refreshing, sweet-tart summer sipper that I can enjoy now *and* later. Doreen's rhubarb used in this recipe is truly the gift that keeps on giving.

The beauty of rhubarb slush is that it makes a large batch, perfect for storing in an ice cream bucket in the freezer. All summer (and sometimes into fall, if I pace myself) I chip away at it whenever I need a cool, nostalgic pick-me-up. I even take it up a notch by making "boozicles"—freezer pops with a grown-up twist—perfect for barbecues, pool parties, or our neighborhood's legendary alley gatherings.

This slush isn't just a treat; it holds a special place in my heart, especially because of the memories it carries. My mom and I spent many summer nights enjoying it together on the deck of my parents' home in Cloquet. After my dad passed, those moments became even more meaningful— our little "happy hour" ritual, a sip of summer and lighter days.

FILLS 1 ICE CREAM PAIL, ABOUT 25 SERVINGS

8 cups sliced rhubarb

8 cups water

3 cups sugar

½ cup freshly squeezed lemon juice

1 (3-ounce) package strawberry Jell-O

2 cups vodka or other liquor, optional

lemon-lime soda, ginger ale, or sparkling water

fresh basil for garnish

Add rhubarb, water, sugar, and lemon juice to large saucepan set over medium heat. Cook, stirring occasionally, until rhubarb is tender, about 20 minutes. Strain the juice into a mixing bowl; discard solids. Stir in in Jell-O and liquor of choice (if using). Transfer to large freezer bags or an ice cream pail. Freeze overnight.

When ready to enjoy, add some to a glass and top with a sparkling beverage or soda of your choice. Garnish with fresh basil.

tip To make boozicles, you'll need plastic Popsicle sleeves with zip seals. The easiest way to fill the sleeves is to prop them in a tall glass or vase and use a turkey baster to transfer the slush from the bucket or bowl into each sleeve. Fill about ¾ inch from the top; the liquid will expand during freezing. Seal and place in freezer for 3–4 hours.

Buffalo Chicken Dip

Chris &
Christine Sarkinen
St. Michael, MN

the dish

A slam dunk of a dip that's a surefire people pleaser and perfect for a potluck.

the tell

When my husband, Jaye, and I helped coordinate the Gustavus swim and dive team's family potlucks during our daughter's swimming years, we were consistently amazed by the bounty of family-favorite recipes that would show up. These dishes weren't just meals; many were treasured traditions, served up in an eclectic mix of well-loved Crock-Pots and sleek, modern slow cookers.

One of the most impressive setups I have ever laid eyes on was the Sarkinen family's legendary Buffalo chicken dip. It was served from a triple slow cooker buffet server and accompanied by chips and a colorful display of bell peppers and cucumbers.

Christine and Chris, parents to two competitive swimmers, knew the importance of fueling a team after a grueling meet. Signing up to bring a generously sized dish was second nature. What they didn't anticipate was just how much of a phenomenon their dip would become.

"The first time we brought it to the Gustavus potluck we had no idea it would be such a hit," Christine recalls. "It just became a thing. Swimmers would ask our kids if we'd be at the meet—and if we were bringing the dip. Parents would spot us and also ask if we brought it." The demand for the dip extended beyond the potluck table, with many of the swimmers taking extra portions back to their room and later going out of their way to tell Christine and Chris how much they enjoyed it.

Christine says the recipe came from a friend who brought it to a potluck several years ago at the school where her husband, Chris, teaches. Over the years it became a staple in their home—a go-to for gatherings and even a comforting après-ski snack. They have fond memories of enjoying the dip after long days on the slopes. Christine's father, who skied up until the age of eighty, looked forward to sharing it with the family after a day in the snow. "My children have always skied with their grandfather, and this is something he loves to have as a snack after skiing," Christine shares. "It's very much a family-and-friends dish."

And now, thanks to the Gustavus swimmers, it's also a team tradition—a dish that started in one kitchen, made its way to countless potlucks, and earned a loyal following along the way.

MAKES ABOUT 3 CUPS, SERVES ABOUT 10

- 2 cups shredded rotisserie chicken or drained canned chicken
- 1 cup mayonnaise
- 1 cup shredded Colby Jack cheese
- ¼ cup blue cheese crumbles
- ¼ cup Buffalo wings hot sauce (Frank's), plus more to taste

for serving: chips and raw vegetables

Stir together chicken, mayonnaise, cheeses, and hot sauce in a slow cooker and heat on low for about 2 hours. Serve with chips and veggies of choice.

tips Christine's family prefers to serve this dip with Fritos scoops and sliced bell peppers (red, orange, and yellow) and cucumbers.

It's an easy recipe to "plus up." Christine says they probably make ten times the recipe for their triple slow cookers.

just for fun Christine says: "My recipe box has been a running joke in the family. It was my grandma's and my mom's, and somehow I wound up with it. The majority of the recipes I don't even make. So when someone looks alphabetically for a recipe and is unable to find it, I always say 'It's in the front.' The recipes I use all get stood up the long way and literally are filed in front of the A!"

Sue's Dip

Sue Miggler
St. Paul, MN

the dish

Creamy, cheesy, and with a slight kick from the picante sauce—this addictive dip is perfect for a potluck or party.

the tell

Sue, who is mom to our good friend and neighbor Dan, is celebrated for the dip she has been bringing to parties and potlucks for the twenty-plus years I have known her. As a matter of fact, most of the times I've seen her throughout the years, she's usually had this glorious dip in tow.

"Sue's Dip," as we call it in our circle, is a tasty concoction of equal parts cream cheese, sour cream, Pace Picante Sauce, and shredded cheese. Seriously, it doesn't get any easier than this dip recipe.

Sue recalls getting the recipe from a coworker many years ago at an office potluck. She worked at a credit union in St. Paul and fondly remembers get-togethers when staff would bring in a variety of crowd-pleasing dishes. These were often cherished, family-favorite recipes and included everything from cocktail meatballs (yes, the kind with grape jelly) to sloppy joes, hotdishes, and, of course, this dip.

From the moment Sue laid eyes (and lips) on this dip at that office potluck years ago, she knew she had to make it. "It's just a great recipe because it's so easy," says Sue. "It takes two minutes to make."

And she has made it over and over again, to the delight of her friends and family and my neighborhood, where she is always a welcome guest—and I swear it is not just because she often brings this dip. Sue is a truly delightful human being; I've always loved catching up with her at our neighbor gatherings... usually as I hover over her beloved dip.

SERVES 20

8 ounces cream cheese, at room temperature

8 ounces sour cream

8 ounces picante sauce (hot or medium)

8 ounces shredded cheddar cheese

for serving: tortilla chips

In a large bowl, blend together the cream cheese, sour cream, and picante sauce. Fold in the cheese. Serve with tortilla chips.

tips

Pace brand picante sauce works best for this dip. Sue uses the hot variety if she is serving the dip to mostly adults but has also used a combination of hot and medium to tone down the heat.

Soften the cream cheese a bit for a smoother dip.

Add garnishes like black olives.

The dip is best served with tortilla chips, but any chip or cracker will work too.

Salami Chips

the dish

Oven-baked salami chips make for crispy and delicious little dippers.

the tell

Sometimes it's the simplest of recipes that make the biggest impression. My mom, Carol, may have understood this truism better than anyone when a few of her fuss-free recipes ended up being the sleeper hits of the potluck table.

When these "chips" debuted at one of the Peterson Fourth of July parties, I remember the reaction, which initially involved many of us scratching our heads. Carol arrived with her usual armloads of contributions to the annual potluck that included an array of bars, cookies, and cupcakes. She couldn't bring just one thing, and sweets were her jam.

But there was one large Tupperware container that typically housed sweets but now contained what appeared to be rows of meat cookies. Imagine our surprise when my mom told us they were chips—made by simply baking slices of salami in the oven. At first no one seemed particularly excited about the meaty morsels. But any doubt about chips made from salami soon disappeared—along with the entire contents of the container they arrived in.

Served with a side of sour cream and freshly torn basil, salami chips proved to be an unexpected hit. Crunchy, salty, and the perfect dipping vessel, they became a party staple in no time. Every year after that, people didn't just hope Carol would bring them—they *expected* it. Funny how something so simple can turn into a legend of its own.

SERVES 5

1 (4-ounce) bag thin-sliced hard salami (Applegate Uncured Genoa Salami)

fresh basil

sour cream

Heat oven to 350 degrees.

Spread salami slices on a parchment-lined baking sheet. Bake for 10–12 minutes, until crisp and browned. Let chips cool and then blot with a paper towel. Garnish with basil and serve with sour cream or other preferred dip. Refrigerate leftover chips in an airtight container.

BLT Bites

the dish

Perky and poppable, these little bites feature the flavors of a BLT and make for a pretty appetizer.

the tell

Another of my mom's memorable contributions to the Peterson July Fourth potlucks (see page 115) was BLT bites—cherry tomatoes stuffed with a mixture of mayo, green onion, bacon, and Parmesan cheese. I believe she brought them to the party only once—probably because they can be a little cumbersome to make. My mom didn't allow herself many kitchen gadgets, so I am certain she used a small paring knife to cut the tops off dozens of bitty tomatoes and then carefully scooped out the pulp. When I first made this recipe in the same fashion, I got so frustrated that I ended up chopping up the tomatoes and turning the recipe into a BLT dip.

While the dip was delicious, I came back to the original recipe once I discovered I could use a mini strawberry huller/tomato corer to gently twist and pull out the pulp. This recipe is now a summer staple I bring to potlucks and look forward to making when it's tomato season and everyone I know seems to have an abundance of garden tomatoes to share with me.

tip A deviled egg tray is the perfect serving dish for this appetizer. You can nestle two to three BLT bites in each egg well, which keeps them from rolling around.

SERVES 10–12

2 pints cherry tomatoes

1 pound bacon, cooked and crumbled

½ cup mayonnaise

⅓ cup chopped green onion

3 tablespoons grated Parmesan cheese

2 tablespoons chopped parsley

Cut the top off the tip of each tomato. Using a small strawberry huller or tomato corer, gently scoop out and discard the pulp, then place the tomatoes upside down on a paper towel to drain excess juice. Combine the remaining ingredients in a bowl, stirring to mix. Using the huller or ¼ teaspoon, scoop the mixture into the tomatoes. Refrigerate until ready to serve.

Sandwich Loaf

the dish

An ingenious way to serve a multilayered sandwich featuring various flavorful spreads, frosted with cream cheese.

the tell

My love for sandwich loaf dates back to experiencing it in all its glory at baby and bridal showers and other ladylike events when I was growing up. The menu for these types of affairs often included an array of fruit and Jell-O salads, dainty finger sandwiches, various bars, nuts, and cream cheese mints—all served on pretty glass luncheon plates, the kind with a little groove for your mug.

These events called for food that was as beautiful as it was delicious, and the sandwich loaf was always the belle of the ball. With its oblong shape and piped "frosting" in pastel-colored flowers, it was a sight to behold and could be easily mistaken for wedding cake.

That's exactly what happened when my friend Toni served one at her wedding as part of an impressive buffet of homemade specialties contributed by her aunts and family. My husband, expecting a bite of cake, was caught off guard when he tasted tuna, ham, chicken, and egg salads. We still laugh about it to this day.

Sandwich loaf may not be for everyone, particularly those expecting something sweet, but I can't think of a more festive way to serve sandwiches featuring various tasty spreads. It's a perfect centerpiece for showers and special celebrations.

Thankfully, Toni shares my obsession. Every spring, leading up to Mother's Day, we get together to make mini sandwich loaves for the special ladies in our lives—as well as for us. We do love eating it almost as much as making it.

We order the long, narrow bread called a Pullman loaf from our hometown supermarket's bakery and get three flavors: molasses rye, white, and wheat, and make a variety of fillings: curry chicken salad, egg salad, tuna salad, and pimento cheese spread. The beauty of sandwich loaf is that you can customize the layers with different breads or whatever fillings you want.

Our favorite part comes after building the sandwich loaf layer by layer and encasing it in cream cheese, when we get down to decorating. Instead of trying to mimic a bakery-style cake, we use bell peppers, cherry tomatoes, radishes, chives, parsley, and olives to create vibrant flowers, butterflies, and whimsical patterns.

"Sandwich loaf is so fun to create and not complicated at all. When you put layers of your favorite spreads on one or several types of bread, it's gratifying when you look at the first slice," says Toni. "They're so pretty and delicious. I love the nostalgia of it all the most. I imagine the ladies who inspired me with this art of sandwich creativity."

It's fun to share this tradition with a longtime friend, and we love spreading the joy of sandwich loaf to others who appreciate its charm—its tasty and distinct layers, nostalgic beauty, and the fun of creating something so delightfully retro. »

Sandwich Loaf

MAKES 1 LOAF; SERVES 18–20

3 (8-ounce) packages whipped cream cheese, at room temperature

½ cup milk or half-and-half

1 loaf Pullman bread, sliced horizontally (ask your local bakery to slice it for you)

garnishes for decorating: berries, radishes, cherry tomatoes, black or green olives, bell peppers, chives, green onion, parsley

egg salad

12 hard-boiled eggs, chopped

¼ cup chopped celery

½ cup mayonnaise

2 tablespoons whole-grain mustard

1 tablespoon sweet relish

1 tablespoon minced dill or chives

salt and pepper, to taste

Place chopped eggs in a large bowl and add celery, mayonnaise, mustard, sweet relish, and dill or chives. Stir to combine and season with salt and pepper to taste.

pimento cheese spread

3 cups coarsely grated extra-sharp cheddar cheese

⅓ cup mayonnaise

6 ounces garlic and herb cream cheese

2 (4-ounce) jars diced pimentos, drained well

1 jalapeño, finely chopped, optional

½ teaspoon onion powder

¼ teaspoon cayenne pepper

salt and pepper, to taste

Mix all ingredients together, stirring to combine.

tuna salad

1 large (11-ounce) and 1 small (6-ounce) pouch tuna in water, drained

½ small red onion, finely chopped

juice from ½ lemon

⅓ cup mayonnaise

½ teaspoon garlic powder

½ teaspoon celery salt

¼ teaspoon pepper

fresh dill to taste

Mix all ingredients together, stirring well and adding more mayo if desired.

curry chicken salad

3 cups shredded cooked chicken

¼ cup finely chopped red onion

2 ribs celery, finely chopped

¼ cup golden raisins

½ cup mayonnaise

2 teaspoons curry powder

1 teaspoon honey

1 teaspoon Dijon mustard

1 tablespoon dry white wine or white grape juice

salt and pepper, to taste

Combine chicken, onion, celery, and raisins in a bowl.

For the dressing, in a medium bowl, combine mayonnaise, curry powder, honey, mustard, and white wine or grape juice. Stir to combine and season with salt and pepper to taste. Add to chicken mixture and stir to mix well.

building the sandwich loaf

After you've made all the spreads and prepped the garnishes, make the frosting by blending cream cheese with a little milk or half-and-half until it reaches desired consistency.

Using 4–6 pieces of bread, depending on how many layers you want, start building your sandwich loaf. (Save extra bread and the top/bottom crust for making breadcrumbs or to feed the birds.) Lay one piece of bread on a serving platter, then spread one of the salads on top. Continue to stack bread and fillings, alternating layers as you go.

Use the cream cheese mixture to frost the loaf as you would a cake, starting with a crumb layer and gradually adding more cream cheese until the loaf is completely covered. If you have extra cream cheese, you could pipe it along the bottom of the loaf and/or edges like a bakery cake. Use garnishes to create fun designs. The possibilities are endless.

Store in refrigerator until ready to serve.

tips The best bread for sandwich loaves is a Pullman loaf, the rectangular sandwich bread that has perfectly square slices: Order it from a bakery and get it pre-sliced. Be sure to specify you want it sliced horizontally.

If you can't get a Pullman loaf, you could order or make sandwich bread and slice it horizontally.

For a smaller or mini sandwich loaf, cut the Pullman loaf into halves or thirds.

While you could use one flavor of bread throughout, we like to use different breads so every bite is unique.

Some people butter the bread on each layer before spreading the filling, to help create a barrier for moisture so the bread doesn't get too soggy.

Layered Tortellini Salad

the dish

A stunner of a salad that combines the flavors of a BLT with a layer of tortellini and creates a beautiful mosaic of color and texture.

the tell

Layered tortellini salad is my go-to dish when I need something a little "showy." It's perfect for special occasions like baby or bridal showers that call for something with a bit of extra pizzazz. I first encountered this gem back in my post-college years, a time filled with celebrations, from bridal showers to baby showers and everything in between. What fun it was to gather and celebrate with friends during such milestone moments in our lives. These events always had an interesting spread of small bites or finger foods and "pretty" salads.

My friend's mother made this salad for one such occasion, and I remember how beautiful it was, served in a low glass casserole so all the layers were visible. Crisp spinach, purple-red cabbage, juicy cherry tomatoes, golden pillows of pasta, and crispy bacon come together for a striking presentation, topped off with a drizzle of ranch dressing.

I am thankful I scored the recipe: I have made it for various showers I've hosted through the years, and it's a salad everyone seems to love. It's substantial enough to stand on its own as a meal but also pairs well with other dishes. I like to serve it in a glass bowl or trifle dish, but I have also used a glass 9x13–inch casserole dish. Either way, the salad's bold, colorful layers will shine through.

Beyond showers and celebrations, I love making this salad for casual summer gatherings and potlucks. It is easy to prepare ahead of time, feeds a crowd, and brings a variety of textures and flavors, making for a great way to round out a buffet. Whether you're hosting an elegant affair or a laid-back gathering, this salad contributes beauty and flavor to the table and will leave a lasting impression.

SERVES 10–12

1 (19-ounce) package cheese tortellini

2 (6-ounce) packages baby spinach

salt and pepper

6 cups shredded red cabbage

1 pint cherry tomatoes, halved, a few reserved for garnish

3 tablespoons green onions, sliced thin

1 pound bacon, cooked and chopped, some pieces reserved for garnish

1 (8-ounce) container ranch or buttermilk dressing

Cook tortellini according to package instructions. Drain and rinse with cold water.

In a large glass bowl, trifle dish, or 9x-13–inch glass baking dish, layer ingredients in this order: spinach sprinkled with salt and pepper, cabbage sprinkled with salt and pepper, tomatoes, green onion, tortellini, bacon. Drizzle with dressing. Garnish with reserved bacon and tomatoes on top. Cover and refrigerate until ready to serve.

tips Omit the bacon or offer it on the side if you are serving this salad at a get-together that includes vegetarians.

I prefer Litehouse Buttermilk Ranch dressing for this salad, but you could certainly make your own.

Dill Pickle Pasta Salad

Marie Mergenthal
Mankato, MN

Staci Mergenthal
Verdi, MN

the dish

A dill-icious salad that involves soaking the pasta in pickle juice overnight for a pickle-y punch.

the tell

You know you are in for something good when the buzz about someone's dish precedes its appearance at the potluck. That's just what happened when word got out that Staci's mother-in-law, Marie, was bringing her dill pickle pasta salad to a Fourth of July gathering several years ago. It's a dish originally created and made viral by Holly Nilsson of the popular blog *Spend With Pennies*, but one that found its way into the hearts (and taste buds) of Marie's family.

In addition to being a fabulous home cook, Marie is the kind of woman who knows how to cook for a crowd, creating dishes packed with flavor and, most importantly, made with love. She has a knack for sensing exactly what will be a hit at family gatherings, and this pasta salad is no exception.

Staci recalls the excitement building as everyone talked about how Marie was bringing two versions of the popular pasta salad, one spicy and one regular, to the party. In addition to small pasta shells and diced dill pickles, Marie's dill pickle pasta salad includes cheddar cheese, white onion, fresh dill, and optional cayenne pepper for a little kick. "It is a bit unexpected, but all the flavors just go together," says Staci, for whom it was love at first bite, not surprising since she likes dill pickles and loves pasta salads. "It was kind of like, how did I not have this in my life already?"

Staci, who shares my passion for handed-down recipes, has a blog called *Random Sweets* and the delightful podcast *Funeral Potatoes and Wool Mittens*, in which she interviews passionate home cooks throughout the Midwest. She interviewed her mother-in-law in 2023 about their family's food traditions, discussing many of Marie's signature specialties, including the dill pickle pasta salad and her special method for packing a pickle-y punch.

In the podcast Marie shares how she boils the pasta al dente and then soaks it overnight, up to twelve hours, in the juice from a jar of pickles. The pasta shells absorb the liquid, and the extended soaking time is what gives the final dish its robust, tangy flavor. "That wasn't something I picked up in a recipe, [it's] something I devised myself," Marie told Staci. "It's my spin on an ordinary pasta salad. Sometimes it's the little details that make all the difference."

Those little details are what set Marie's cooking apart. She has a deep-rooted understanding of flavors and a heart for feeding her family and friends with comforting, delicious meals. Her dishes aren't just sustenance: They're an experience, a memory, and a way of bringing people together. It's the type of advice Staci appreciates from her mother-in-law, who is known in her family for showing her love by cooking for others.

Staci says Marie's dill pickle pasta salad is a great dish for a party or potluck as it can be made ahead and stands out from other salads typically found at Midwestern gatherings. "It's definitely different. You either love it or you hate it, but most people who like pickles will love it."

SERVES 10

8 ounces small or medium shell pasta

juice from 1 (25- to 32-ounce) jar pickles

⅔ cup mayonnaise

⅓ cup sour cream

2 tablespoons chopped dill

⅛ teaspoon cayenne pepper, optional

¾ cup sliced baby dill pickles or finely chopped pickle chips

⅔ cup cubed sharp cheddar cheese

3 tablespoons finely chopped white onion

Cook pasta shells al dente according to package instructions. Drain and rinse pasta in cold water. Place pasta in a bowl with pickle juice and stir to combine. Cover bowl tightly and place in refrigerator overnight or about 12 hours.

Drain pasta well. In a small bowl, stir together mayonnaise, sour cream, dill, and cayenne pepper (if using). Add to the pasta and stir to coat completely. Stir in the pickles, cheese, and onion. For best flavor, cover and refrigerate 8–12 hours before serving.

tips

Plan ahead: This recipe is best when the pasta soaks in pickle juices for twelve hours. Marie also recommends refrigerating the assembled salad for eight to twelve hours.

This versatile recipe can be modified to your preference. If you prefer sweet pickles, for example, use sweet pickles and celery seed instead of dill pickles and dill. Different pickles will result in a different texture. While Marie uses baby dill pickles or gherkins, Staci prefers dill pickle chips.

Experiment with different pasta shapes and sizes. The original recipe calls for small shells, but Staci prefers the medium ones, "just big enough for the pickles and the cheese to slide into the shells so you get a perfect bite with all the ingredients."

Add a little protein by serving chicken, salami, or summer sausage on the side.

Crunchy Coleslaw

Julie Peterson
St. Louis Park, MN

the dish

A toasty twist on crunchy coleslaw made with ramen noodles and slivered almonds.

the tell

The term *salad* has some loose interpretations when it comes to Midwest potlucks. Many so-called salads lean closer to desserts for their use of ingredients such as Jell-O, cookies, or candy bars, but one standout is a true coleslaw from a family friend, Julie, that's always a crowd favorite. "Whenever Julie brings this coleslaw to potluck gatherings, everyone loves it and it disappears fast," says my sister-in-law Kara of the "crunchy coleslaw" that includes ramen noodles and slivered almonds.

Julie, who admits she isn't big on cooking, appreciates the simplicity of the recipe and that it makes a large bowl to feed a crowd. "I also like the crunch from the ramen noodles and how it is a somewhat healthier dish to bring to a potluck."

I've encountered (and enjoyed) variations of this coleslaw through the years, including one my mom used to make with cashews and sunflower seeds. What sets Julie's version apart is that she toasts the ramen noodles and almonds, which boosts the overall flavor and texture of the dish. The result is a light and delightfully crunchy salad that brings a nice balance to some of the more indulgent dishes that are often part of a potluck spread.

SERVES ABOUT 20

salad

- **noodles from 2 (3-ounce) packages ramen noodle soup, soy sauce flavor**
- **1 tablespoon oil**
- **1 cup slivered almonds**
- **2 (14-ounce) bags coleslaw**
- **1–2 bunches green onion, chopped (about 1½ cups)**

dressing

- **½ cup olive oil**
- **¼ cup vinegar**
- **1 tablespoon soy sauce**
- **⅓ cup sugar**
- **flavor packets from the ramen noodle packages**

Break the noodles into bite-size pieces. Heat oil in a skillet and toast ramen noodles and almonds until light brown. Set aside.

In a large bowl, stir together dressing ingredients. Just before serving, toss coleslaw mix, onions, noodles, and almonds with the dressing.

just for fun Julie has her mom's recipe box, which contains many recipes in her mom's writing, including the family's recipe for sandbakkels, which Julie continues to make each year with her sister for the holidays.

Julie also has her grandma's spice cabinet and a cutting board with her mom's chili recipe engraved on it.

tips This salad is best when fresh, so Julie suggests mixing it together right before serving. You can prep the dressing and toast the noodles and almonds beforehand.

Add some chicken for a little protein.

Sweet Memories

Here's what's cookin'

Mom's One & Only Chocolate Cake 131
Elaine's Pineapple Upside-Down Cake 134
Becky's Birthday Cake 137
Rum Cake 140
Self-Filled Cupcakes 142
Chocolate Chip Shortbread Cookies 144

Here's what's cookin'

Molasses Crinkle Cookies 147
Aunt Sally Cookies 149
Grandma Janet's White Cookies 151
Jan's Club Cracker Bars 154
Toffee Bars 157
Thunderstorm Bars 158
Rhubarb Pie Bars 161
Rhubarb Meringue Dessert 164
Frozen Strawberry Dessert 166
Peanut Butter Pie 169
Homemade Chocolate Pudding 170
Betty's Caramels 173

Many recipes from the heart are the sweet treats and baked goods that transport us back to childhood. From Grandma's cookies stored in a coffee tin to a birthday cake made with love to a decadent dessert shared at special gatherings, these sweet treats are often core memories, tied to a specific moment in time or a particular loved one.

This rings true for me as one of my earliest memories is standing alongside my mom in the kitchen as she baked one of her signature sweets, which she did often. Whether it was chocolate chip shortbread cookies, toffee bars, or the chocolate cake she'd make for our birthdays, I would be assigned certain tasks, such as chopping nuts or "cleaning" the beaters from the electric mixer (that is, licking them clean). But mostly I would stand quietly and observe her in action, waiting for when the cookies or other treats were done baking, watching through the window in the oven, and eagerly anticipating the moment we could sample the results of my mom's hard work.

In my preteen years I received my first cookbook, *The New Junior Cookbook* from Better Homes and Gardens, and was allowed to bake snickerdoodles on my own—a significant rite of passage that likely sparked my love of baking and a fondness for these cinnamon sugar–dusted cookies. This one remains a go-to recipe whenever I want an easy, no-frills sweet treat to remind me of home. I also love any opportunity to revisit this relic of a cookbook that's a reminder of simpler times and growing up in the eighties.

I relish learning about other families' treasured treats, whether it is a favorite bar requested for family gatherings such as Jan's Club Cracker bars or a special cake that is baked once a year, like Becky's birthday cake. And no surprise, many of these adored treats trace back to grandmothers: homemade chocolate pudding, pineapple upside-down cake, Betty's caramels, and an array of cookies—molasses, sour cream cutouts, and Aunt Sallys, to name a few!

This chapter offers a tribute to those sweet memories—the simple joys found in flour, sugar, and butter, and the act of baking a favorite treat with or for the ones you love.

Mom's One & Only Chocolate Cake

the dish

The little black dress of chocolate cakes.

the tell

Just like every woman should have a little black dress in her closet, all home cooks need a recipe for a great chocolate cake—one you can feel confident reaching for when the occasion calls for it, knowing it will look perfect and taste amazing every time.

In my family our LBD or, as we call it, "the one and only chocolate cake" is a recipe my mom, Carol, has been making for the past fifty years. It's rich and decadent and oh-so-chocolatey, thanks in part to the cup of hot coffee added to the batter to intensify the flavor. It's also encased in a thick, velvety layer of—you guessed it—more chocolate in the form of a rich buttercream frosting.

This cake has taken center stage at our family birthday celebrations for as long as I can remember. I loved these special occasions, for the extra guests like my grandparents and neighbors seated around our table, for the presents and all the attention on me (when it was my birthday), but most of all for "the cake"!

My mom would pull out all the stops, serving the cake on a drop-dead-gorgeous crystal Fostoria cake stand that my parents got as a wedding gift in 1967. The cake would arrive on the table in all its glory and immediately be greeted with oohs and aahs before the ceremonial slicing and serving, always with a hefty side of ice cream. Chocolate chip, vanilla, or Neapolitan were our typical options and remain our favorites to accompany this cake.

These days when we are lucky enough to gather together for a family birthday, we don't even have to ask what kind of cake there will be. We know. It wouldn't be a birthday celebration without my mom's one and only chocolate cake. »

Mom's One & Only Chocolate Cake

SERVES 12–15

cake

2 cups flour

2 cups sugar

¾ cup cocoa

2 teaspoons baking soda

1 teaspoon baking powder

1 teaspoon salt

1 cup vegetable oil

1 cup hot coffee

1 cup milk

2 eggs

1 teaspoon vanilla

buttercream frosting

1½ cups (3 sticks) butter, at room temperature

1 cup cocoa

5 cups powdered sugar, sifted

½ cup milk

2 teaspoons vanilla

for the cake

Heat oven to 325 degrees. Grease and flour 2 (9-inch) cake pans.

In a large mixing bowl, sift together dry ingredients. Add oil, coffee, and milk; mix at medium speed until combined. Add eggs and vanilla; beat again. Batter will be thin.

Pour batter into prepared cake pans and bake 25–30 minutes, until an inserted toothpick or cake tester comes out clean. Cool cakes at least 15 minutes before removing from pans.

for the buttercream frosting

In a mixing bowl, combine the butter and cocoa, mixing well. Add 1 cup of powdered sugar followed by 1 tablespoon of milk. Mix at high speed for 1 minute. Add remaining powdered sugar, 1 cup at a time with 1 tablespoon of milk, until all the sugar has been added. You may need more or less milk depending on desired consistency. Add vanilla and stir to combine.

Spread frosting on cooled cake layers.

tips When greasing and flouring the cake pans, use cocoa powder instead of flour.

For a little twist, make vanilla buttercream tinted with food coloring for the inside layer of the cake. It makes for a pretty surprise when cutting into the cake and strikes a nice balance with the chocolate.

Elaine's Pineapple Upside-Down Cake

Nikki Theis-Mahon
St. Paul, MN

the dish

A classic pineapple upside-down cake with caramelized brown sugar, golden pineapple rings, and bright cherries.

the tell

My neighbor Nikki makes an old-fashioned pineapple upside-down cake that is not only delicious but also a true dazzler—just like the recipe's namesake, her grandma Elaine. Elaine was Nikki's "fancy" grandma, who was rarely seen without her nylon stockings and Love that Pink lipstick, even for a day at home. Nikki recalls stories about how Elaine and her sister would wear matching dresses on Christmas Eve and serve identical hotdishes. In a bit of sisterly rivalry, they'd cheekily poll guests on who looked the best and whose hotdish was better!

But when it came to desserts, there was no contest. Elaine's pineapple upside-down cake, with caramelized brown sugar and a pretty patterned topping of pineapple rings and cherries, created a beautiful showstopper.

For Nikki, the cake is not just a recipe; it's a special connection to her family. It was her late father's favorite, baked by her grandma Elaine every year for his birthday. Now, as the keeper of this cherished tradition, Nikki bakes it a few times a year—sometimes for potlucks, sometimes just because she needs cake or a slice of nostalgia. "I think pineapple upside-down cake is a stunner and I love its mid-century appeal," says Nikki. She also appreciates how the recipe relies on simple pantry staples, making it an easy go-to treat any time.

And what a treat it is! The brown sugar topping melts into the golden cake, creating a rich, caramelized flavor that perfectly complements the fruit. The cake itself is sturdy enough to hold the pineapple yet airy enough to feel light and luscious. Whether shared over coffee with a neighbor or served at a celebration, it's the kind of dessert that brightens any room—just like Elaine surely did. »

Elaine's Pineapple Upside-Down Cake

SERVES 12

4 tablespoons butter, plus ⅓ cup butter, at room temperature

2 eggs, separated

1½ cups flour

1 tablespoon baking powder

¼ teaspoon salt

⅔ cup granulated sugar

1 teaspoon vanilla

⅔ cup water

1 cup packed brown sugar

1 (20-ounce) can pineapple rings, drained

20 maraschino cherries

Heat oven to 350 degrees. Place 4 tablespoons butter in 9-inch round or 9x9–inch square pan and set in the oven to melt. Beat egg whites to soft peaks (see tip); set aside. In a separate bowl, sift together flour, baking powder, and salt; set aside.

In a large mixing bowl, combine ⅓ cup butter and granulated sugar, mixing well. Beat in egg yolks and vanilla. Alternate adding dry ingredients and water, mixing well after each addition. Fold in egg whites.

Remove pan from the oven and stir brown sugar in melted butter until dissolved. Arrange pineapple rings with cherries in their center on butter–sugar mixture. Pour batter on top.

Bake for 35–40 minutes or until an inserted toothpick or cake tester comes out clean.

Cool cake on a rack for 20 minutes. Invert over a serving plate and gently remove the pan.

tips Melt the butter right in the baking pan as the oven preheats, then add the brown sugar. Be sure the sugar fully dissolves.

The recipe calls for separating the eggs and whisking the egg whites until fluffy. Nikki advises to make sure your bowl is absolutely clean with no grease or residue. The goal is a consistency where the eggs cling to the whisk and droop slightly off the end — not too stiff.

just for fun For one of Nikki's wedding showers, guests were asked to bring a favorite recipe on a card. "One card was even typed — I was impressed!" she says. "It was such a thoughtful gift and a great way to share beloved dishes."

Nikki credits her culinary curiosity to weekends spent watching Julia Child and Jacques Pépin with her parents. "We only had one TV, so if I wanted to watch something, I watched what they were watching. I didn't realize how much I absorbed until I was cooking on my own."

The oldest items in Nikki's kitchen are her Griswold cast iron pans from the late 1920s–30s. "We use them weekly — for grilled cheese, cornbread, skillet cookies. They're high quality and built to last."

Nikki loves her collection of vintage Tupperware cake and pie carriers, which are both pretty and practical.

Becky's Birthday Cake

Becky Brandt
Long Lake, MN

the dish

A true celebration cake made from layers of angel food and pretty sherbet, frosted with whipped topping, and adorned with M&M's.

the tell

As long as Becky can remember, her birthdays have included a very special cake thanks to the creativity of her mom, Karen. This spectacular showstopper of a cake is piled high with thick sherbet spread in between three layers of angel food cake and topped with fluffy whipped topping and colorful M&M candies, but that's not all. It's a sweet tradition that has endured even after Karen's passing and is an everlasting reminder of a mom's love.

Known in the family as "Becky's Angel Food Birthday Cake," it was something that Becky's mom made special, just for her, starting when Becky was two or three years old. Becky is unsure of the recipe's origins but notes her mom was a passionate home cook who loved baking. "She was always trying new recipes and took pride in making food for others," says Becky, who recalls many fun memories of spending time in the kitchen with her mom.

After her mom died in 2014, Becky was feeling sad as her birthday approached and at the thought of not having the special cake ever again. However, her husband surprised her by reaching out to a bakery and asking them to re-create the cake that had brought so much joy to Becky her whole life. Becky loved and appreciated the gesture but admitted it wasn't quite the same as her mom's homemade version.

A few years later, Becky's daughter Alissa, who was ten years old at the time, snuck over to the neighbor's to re-create the cake exactly from Karen's recipe and surprise Becky with it on her birthday. "I'm rarely surprised, but it was so sweet," says Becky. "She has done it every year since." Becky is touched that her family recognizes the sentimental value of the cake, although she jokes that her kids don't enjoy eating it nearly as much as she does. "I like this recipe because it's light and refreshing and not overpoweringly sweet," says Becky. "I've always loved ice cream cakes, too: It's like two treats in one." »

Becky's Birthday Cake

SERVES 10–12

1 (9-inch) angel food cake (store-bought or homemade)

2 (16-ounce) pints sherbet, softened

1 (12-ounce) container whipped topping (Cool Whip), softened

M&M's

Make room in your freezer to fit the cake while assembling the layers and to store the final masterpiece.

Using a serrated knife, cut cake horizontally into 3 sections. Place a base layer on a plate. Spread 1 pint of softened sherbet on top by scooping "chunks" of it onto the cake; the sherbet should be moldable. Place next piece of cake atop the sherbet layer and freeze for 10 minutes.

Remove cake from freezer and spread second layer of softened sherbet as before. Place third cake layer on top and refreeze.

After approximately 15 minutes, quickly spread softened whipped topping all over the cake. Refreeze for 10 minutes and dot with M&M's when whipped topping is refrozen. Serve immediately or put back in the freezer until ready to eat.

tip Stick to the recipe: Keep it classic. Becky's mom tried a few different variations through the years, using cream cheese frosting or making a loaf shape, but always returned to the original.

just for fun In 2013 Becky and her mom took on the task of creating a family cookbook that includes more than two hundred recipes. It was a true labor of love that came about when they sought recipe submissions and photos from family members, and it grew to become a beautiful tribute to their rich German and Lebanese heritage. Becky says it's a constant fixture on her counter and she and her family use it regularly.

Sarah's notes

Stock up on different color M&M's when they are in season, e.g., Easter pastels or Valentine's Day reds, or order single colors online to adorn the cake to your liking.

For a taller cake, use more than a pint of sherbet per layer.

Tint the Cool Whip with food coloring for a pretty twist.

Rum Cake

the dish

A beautiful boozy Bundt cake with a buttery rum glaze.

the tell

If there is one recipe I am known for among friends and family, it's this rum cake. But whenever someone asks for the recipe, I have to sheepishly admit that I found it on the internet years ago by searching "best rum cake ever." Then I also have to admit how embarrassingly easy the cake is to make, starting with a boxed cake mix and including a package of pudding mix, a common ingredient in many vintage cake recipes. But despite its origins, this cake has lived up to the hype. I've made it countless times, and whenever I share it people always seem to lose their minds.

Beyond bringing rum cake to potlucks, I always make it for New Year's Eve. With its rich, boozy flavor, it feels like the perfect adults-only celebratory dessert to ring in the new year. Plus, baking it in a Bundt pan makes for a beautiful and dramatic cake that looks like it took far more effort than it actually did. Sometimes I feel guilty using a cake mix, but that's probably what makes this a fairly foolproof recipe, and the addition of rum to the batter and the buttery rum glaze truly set this cake apart from the rest.

When it comes to rum, any dark or spiced rum will do, giving the most flavor bang for your buck over white rum. Our family's personal favorite is Shipwreck rum, which is distilled in the Caribbean. We first discovered it on the island of St. Kitts, my in-laws' wintertime home away from home—a place very near and dear to our hearts. The rum comes in many flavors—coffee, vanilla, mango—and I can attest that they all make for a uniquely delicious and flavorful rum cake.

In sharing this cake and recipe through the years, I've encountered others who claim it is a family favorite or one of their signature dishes as well. Perhaps they also searched the internet for "best rum cake ever"!

tips **Have fun with different styles and sizes of Bundt cake pans. I like to use two smaller, half-size Bundt pans so I have one cake for now and another for later—or one to give away and one to keep. If using two smaller Bundt pans, the cake will bake in about 30–40 minutes.**

To ensure the cake soaks up all the boozy goodness, poke holes in it with a skewer or chopstick while it's still warm before pouring on the glaze.

The longer the cake soaks in the rum, the better. The cake can be left out on the counter for a few days (covered well), refrigerated, or frozen for later enjoyment.

SERVES 12

cake

1 (15.25-ounce) yellow cake mix

1 (3.4-ounce) package instant vanilla pudding mix

4 eggs

½ cup dark rum

½ cup water

½ cup vegetable oil

glaze

½ cup (1 stick) butter

1 cup sugar

¼ cup water

½ cup dark rum

Heat oven to 325 degrees. Grease and flour Bundt pan(s).

In a large bowl, combine cake mix and pudding mix. Mix in eggs, ½ cup rum, ½ cup water, and oil. Pour batter into prepared pan(s). Bake 1 hour for a full-size Bundt pan or 30–40 minutes for 2 smaller Bundt pans or until an inserted toothpick or cake tester comes out clean. Let cake sit in pan for about 10 minutes while you make the glaze.

In a saucepan set over medium heat, melt the butter and stir in sugar and ¼ cup water. Bring to a rapid boil for about 5 minutes. Remove from heat; stir in ½ cup rum.

Carefully remove cake from pan and lightly brush glaze on top and sides of cake. Pour about half of the glaze into the empty Bundt pan and put the cake back in the pan. Use a cake tester, skewer, or chopstick to poke holes in the bottom of the cake, then pour the remaining glaze all over the bottom of the cake and along the sides of the pan. When ready to serve (see tip), remove cake from pan and place on a serving platter.

Self-Filled Cupcakes

the dish

Vanilla cupcakes with a surprise filling of cream cheese and chocolate chips and topped with a rich, chocolate frosting.

the tell

These are my mom's signature cupcakes that she has made for years, to bring to potlucks, to celebrate all sorts of special occasions, and, more often than not, "just because." While they look like ordinary cupcakes, they have a surprise hidden inside: a filling with cream cheese and chocolate chips. This fun, unexpected twist makes these cupcakes seem like they came from a fancy bakery, yet they are so easy to make.

The recipe starts with a cake mix and adds a dollop of the filling to each cupcake before baking. It doesn't get much easier than that. One could cut corners by using store-bought frosting, but my mom's recipe includes a decadent chocolate glaze that is just one more way these cupcakes stand out from the rest.

I've made these cupcakes over and over again throughout the years, and now my daughter, Lucy, makes them too. No matter the occasion, they always evoke oohs and aahs. I love seeing the reaction when someone bites into one. And as long as we keep baking these cupcakes, the surprise inside will never get old—just like the joy of sharing them with the people we love.

MAKES ABOUT 16

cupcakes

1 (13.25-ounce) package white or yellow cake mix, plus oil and/or eggs per package directions

filling

8 ounces cream cheese, at room temperature

⅓ cup sugar

1 egg, beaten

pinch salt

1 cup chocolate chips

frosting

1 cup sugar

⅓ cup milk

5 tablespoons butter

1 cup chocolate chips

Line a muffin tin with cupcake liners. Heat oven and prepare cake mix according to directions on packaging. Set aside.

In a separate bowl, combine cream cheese, ⅓ cup sugar, beaten egg, and salt, mixing well. Stir in 1 cup chocolate chips.

Fill cupcake liners about two-thirds full with cake batter. Drop 1 heaping tablespoon of the cream cheese mixture into each cupcake. Bake as package directs.

For the frosting, in a medium saucepan set over medium heat, combine 1 cup sugar, milk, and butter and bring to boiling; boil for 1 minute. Stir in 1 cup chocolate chips until smooth. Remove from heat. Use a hand mixer to beat frosting until smooth and glossy. Spread frosting on cupcakes while still warm (see tip).

tips The glaze is a little thin, so I like to dip the tops of the cupcakes into a shallow bowl of the frosting to get an even coating.

It's fun to experiment with different flavors of cake mix or tint the inside filling. For instance, I add a bit of orange food coloring to the filling for Halloween cupcakes or pink for Valentine's Day.

Chocolate Chip Shortbread Cookies

the dish

A gussied-up chocolate chip cookie made from tender shortbread and topped with a dusting of powdered sugar.

the tell

The most popular cookie from my mom's recipe box, these chocolate chip shortbread cookies are adored by everyone who encounters them, including the judges at the Minnesota State Fair. They earned me a third-place ribbon in the "light, ball type, flattened before baking" cookie category in 2022. The judges' comments included "great taste" and "they melt in your mouth." I agree! Something about the shortbread makes these cookies a delight to bite into and downright irresistible.

It's a somewhat humble recipe with a short list of ingredients, but don't let that fool you. These little bites of buttery bliss will dazzle on treat trays and stand out on the dessert table at a potluck or shower. Featuring the delicate imprint of fork tines kissed with powdered sugar, the cookies are dainty and delicious.

Thanks to my mom, Carol, these cookies were part of many of our family celebrations and special occasions, and also dispersed around town, as she loved to share her baking. When I returned home to visit in my adult years, it was a welcome sight to find a secret stash in the freezer just for me. Now it's my turn to return the favor, as I like to make them for Mom when I visit.

MAKES ABOUT 5 DOZEN

2 cups (4 sticks) butter, at room temperature

2 cups powdered sugar, plus extra for sprinkling

2 teaspoons vanilla

½ teaspoon salt

4½ cups flour

1 (12-ounce) package semisweet chocolate chips

Heat oven to 350 degrees.

In a large mixing bowl, combine butter and powdered sugar, mixing well. Beat in vanilla and salt. Add flour and mix well. Stir in chocolate chips. Use a cookie scoop or tablespoon to portion the dough into balls; place on an ungreased cookie sheet. Flatten each ball slightly with a fork dipped in powdered sugar.

Bake for 15 minutes. Remove cookies to a cooling rack and sift some powdered sugar on top of cookies while they are still warm.

tips For a smaller, daintier cookie, I use a rounded tablespoon to portion the dough balls.

The recipe makes a lot of cookies, but it's easy to cut it in half or to freeze the cookies for later.

You can make the dough a day ahead. Fun fact: I entered these cookies in the Minnesota State Fair's Blue Ribbon Baking Contest twice before I won a ribbon for them. The one thing I did differently for the award-winning version was to make the cookie dough the day before, refrigerating it overnight.

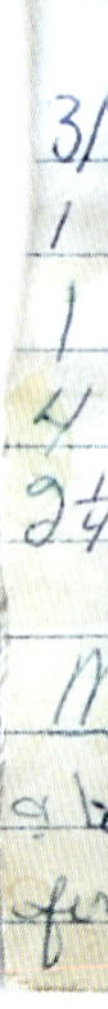

Molasses Crinkle Cookies

Maria Manske
St. Paul, MN

the dish

Sugar, spice, and everything nice.

the tell

These scrumptious molasses cookies, with sugar-dusted crackles, taste and smell like they came straight from the oven of Mrs. Claus. But the recipe isn't from the North Pole—it's an old-fashioned recipe from my friend Maria, whose mom, Helen, baked them for her and her six siblings when they were growing up. The cookies were a beloved staple, tucked into the brown-bag lunches Helen lovingly packed for Maria.

"Helen's cookies were straight-up, perfectly round, crisp masterpieces," says Maria. "No frills, with a sprinkling of sugar—that's all they needed." She notes her mom used Crisco—which results in a nice, round shape and an irresistible, just-right crisp texture. It's true, moms do know best!

Molasses Crinkle Cookies
p shortening } 1/4 tsp. salt
sugar } 2 tsp. soda
g, well beaten } 1/2 tsp cloves
p, molasses } 1 tsp cinnamon
s sifted flour - all purpose } 1 tsp ginger
d - Cream shortening & sugar. Add egg, molasses
ell. Sift together dry ingredients and add to
mixture. Shape into balls (size of a walnut)
(over)

MAKES 2 DOZEN

2¼ cups flour, sifted

2 teaspoons baking soda

1 teaspoon cinnamon

1 teaspoon ginger

½ teaspoon cloves

¼ teaspoon salt

¾ cup vegetable shortening (Crisco)

1 cup sugar, plus more for rolling

1 egg, well beaten

¼ cup molasses

Heat oven to 375 degrees. In a medium bowl, sift together flour, baking soda, cinnamon, ginger, cloves, and salt; set aside.

In a large bowl, combine shortening and sugar, mixing well. Add egg and molasses and beat well. Add dry ingredients to bowl and mix well. Shape into balls about the size of a walnut and roll in sugar. Bake on greased cookie sheets for 12–15 minutes.

just for fun

Maria is lucky to be the keeper of her mom's recipe box, which is chock-full of many family-favorite recipes, including the well-loved recipe card for molasses crinkle cookies.

the dish

Soft molasses cookies cut into a rectangular shape with the help of a can of Spam and topped with a unique white icing that hardens on top.

Amelia Lux
Canton, GA

Patricia Erickson-Mann
Springfield, MO

Aunt Sally Cookies

the tell

A few years ago I was on a mission to find a recipe for Aunt Sally cookies—the gingerbread-like treats with their signature rectangular shape and hardened white icing. I put out a call on my Facebook page, and to my surprise I received a cherished family recipe straight from my husband's great-aunt!

No, her name wasn't Sally; it was Jeanette. Though she passed away in 2017, her granddaughter Amelia reached out to me to share her grandmother's recipe, which was the exact version I was hoping to find, complete with the trick of using a can of Spam to create the classic shape.

Aunt Sally cookies, sometimes referred to as Sally Ann cookies, got their name from a packaged version popular in the 1950s. As more home bakers attempted to do their own re-creations, variations started appearing in church cookbooks—one of which inspired Jeanette's version. Over the years she fine-tuned the recipe to her liking, creating a tradition that continues in her family today.

Jeanette's daughter Patricia shared some fun memories of the cookies and growing up on the family farm in Ross, Minnesota. She remembers her mother making them often as part of her weekly baking routine each Saturday. "We were blessed with fresh bread, buns, cakes, bars, and, of course, cookies on a weekly basis," says Patricia. "There were a lot of mouths to feed, and baking was the most economical way of doing things on the farm."

She adds it was like Grand Central Station at times with all the comings and goings between their family of four children, the hired men who helped on the farm, and all the extended family who would stop in for a visit. "Mother and father were wonderful hosts, always ready with coffee and a homemade treat," says Patricia. She adds that in later years, her own children enjoyed the same royal treatment when they visited the farm. They loved eating freshly baked cookies and donuts at the kitchen table and also sneaking some extra treats from the freezer when no one was looking. "I remember Grandma having a stash of Aunt Sally cookies in her freezer, wrapped in waxed paper, inside an old coffee tin," Amelia reminisces.

Jeanette was also known to send elaborate Christmas care packages to family who lived far away from Roseau County. "Flatbread and cookies were shipped with popcorn used as packing material to ensure everything arrived in good condition," says Patricia. "Lefse and donuts were included as well and, of course, a batch of Aunt Sally cookies. With great anticipation, the box would be opened, unpacked, and inspected with oohs and ahhs."

In 2011 Patricia entered the Aunt Sally cookies in the county fair, where they won first place in the heritage cookie contest.

This recipe is more than just a sweet treat—it's a testament to family, tradition, and the simple joys of sharing something made with love. ➸

Aunt Sally Cookies

MAKES ABOUT 3 DOZEN

cookies

2 teaspoons baking soda

½ cup hot water

6 cups flour

1 teaspoon salt

1 teaspoon ginger

1 teaspoon cinnamon

½ teaspoon allspice

½ teaspoon nutmeg

¼ teaspoon cloves

1 cup (2 sticks) butter, at room temperature

1½ cups granulated sugar

1 cup molasses

icing

1 envelope unflavored gelatin

¾ cup cold water

¾ cup granulated sugar

1¾ cups powdered sugar, sifted

¾ teaspoon vanilla

Add baking soda to hot water, stirring to completely dissolve; set aside. In separate bowl, combine flour, salt, and spices; set aside.

In a mixing bowl, combine butter, sugar, and molasses, mixing well. Add baking soda mixture and stir to combine. Gradually stir in flour mixture until a nice dough forms. Chill for an hour or more.

Heat oven to 375 degrees.

Roll out dough, keeping it somewhat thick. Use a Spam can to cut cookies into the distinctive rectangular shape. Set on cookie sheets and bake for 6–8 minutes. Remove to a rack and cool completely.

For frosting, in a saucepan set over medium heat, combine gelatin and cold water, stirring to dissolve. Stir in granulated sugar and bring to a simmer for 10 minutes.

Place powdered sugar in a separate bowl. Pour sugar–gelatin mixture into powdered sugar and beat until foamy. Add vanilla and beat until thick.

Work fast to frost cookies (see tip).

tips

The dough for these cookies has to be chilled before rolling and cutting. In the winter Jeanette put her dough on the enclosed porch to chill it to the right temperature.

A Spam can makes the perfect cookie cutter to create the oblong shape these cookies are known for. The dough should be rolled out quite thick, about ¼ inch, to get the best texture and shape.

Amelia notes that making the frosting requires patience and, once made, it takes some speed to cover the cookies before the icing sets, but it's worth the effort as the icing is one of the things that makes the cookies so delicious.

Patricia suggests frosting the bottom of the cookie for a flatter surface.

just for fun

Amelia's sisters gave her a beautiful family cookbook as a wedding gift in 2012. Using Shutterfly, the sisters created a 12x12–inch scrapbook-style book that features multigenerational family recipes, including Jeanette's Aunt Sally cookies, and pictures of immediate and extended family members.

Grandma Janet's White Cookies

Staci Mergenthal
Verdi, MN

the dish

A vintage recipe for a melt-in-your-mouth, round white cookie with a sparkly, sugar-dusted top.

the tell

Staci will always cherish the memory of Grandma Janet showing up each Christmas with a plastic pail of round white cookies, their tops glistening with sugar. Carefully packaged, these delicate treats were just as much a holiday staple as they were a hallmark of her grandma's time in the kitchen and one of her signature recipes that the whole family loved.

Today Grandma Janet's white cookies remain a treasured tradition Staci carries forward. She bakes them a few times a year—during the holidays or whenever she wants to share a piece of family history. Beyond the sentimental value, Staci loves their simple yet sophisticated vanilla flavor, perfectly round shape, and twinkly sugar-coated tops. "It's a cookie that's not too sweet, which is why it's easy to eat too many," says Staci, adding that the cookies can be soft or have a crispier texture, depending on how long you bake them. "Each person in my family has a preference, so I bake half of them soft and half crispy. However, both textures have crispy edges with sugared tops that melt in your mouth."

The vintage recipe, passed down from Grandma Janet's mother-in-law, is unique—using sour cream and the rare technique of swelling the baking soda before adding it to the batter. Staci is grateful to have learned the recipe firsthand, baking alongside her grandmother before she passed. "Her recipe didn't include detailed instructions, so I learned by watching her," Staci recalls—a special day of baking she documented on her blog, *Random Sweets*. Adding to the nostalgia, she treasures the baking tools they used that day—her grandmother's trusty Sunbeam Mixmaster, the marbled applewood rolling pin made by her great-grandfather, as well as her grandma's round cookie cutter and sugar shaker. While she still uses most of these heirlooms, the vintage Sunbeam mixer—the oldest item in her kitchen—now sits proudly on display, a cherished reminder of their time spent baking together.

Every time Staci bakes with these tools of the trade, she feels a deep connection to her grandparents, who lived in Brookings, South Dakota, where Staci grew up. She had the chance to visit her grandparents often and develop a close bond with them—especially her grandma—which grew stronger as Staci got older.

In addition to cookies, Grandma Janet preserved their Scandinavian heritage by making lefse, krumkake, sandbakkels, and rosettes. But it's the white cookies that define Christmas for Staci and hold a special place in her heart, bringing back sweet memories—not just of the well-loved cookies but of time baking them with her grandmother and carrying on a cherished family tradition. »

memories

Grandma Janet's White Cookies

MAKES ABOUT 7 DOZEN

1 cup sour cream

1 teaspoon baking soda

2 cups sugar, plus more for sprinkling

1 cup vegetable shortening (Crisco)

2 eggs, at room temperature

1 teaspoon vanilla

6½ cups flour, plus more for rolling

1 teaspoon baking powder

tips Roll out the cookie dough so thin that you think it's too thin.

Staci prefers using a round cookie cutter, the one her grandma used, and notes the cookies don't spread so they bake perfectly round.

just for fun Staci is the proud keeper of Grandma Janet's recipe box, featuring many of her handwritten recipes. Staci also has a beautiful arrangement of some of her grandma's recipes, including the white cookies, framed by her sister.

In addition to Grandma Janet, Staci credits her mom, Linda, and her sisters, Heidi and Kalli, for their influence on her passion for cooking and baking. "My mom's and my grandma's love languages have been baking so I wonder if that's where I got mine."

Staci recalls another favorite cookie from Grandma Janet that made the house smell like "Grandma's house." Mother's Cookies were molasses cookies imprinted with a starburst design from the bottom of a special glass that was a "gift" inside an oatmeal canister, much like toys in a cereal box.

Place sour cream in a bowl and stir in baking soda. Let sit at room temperature for 30 minutes. The sour cream will begin to swell as the soda dissolves.

In a large bowl or the bowl of a stand mixer, beat the sugar and shortening until creamy.

In separate bowl, whisk eggs until well beaten. Add to the sugar mixture and beat on medium-high until combined. Spoon sour cream into the batter and add vanilla. Beat on medium-high for 3 minutes, turning off the mixer a few times to scrape down the sides of the bowl.

In a separate bowl, whisk together flour and baking powder. Add flour to the cookie batter 1 cup at a time, beating on medium-low speed after each addition, until all the flour is incorporated and the dough is stiff.

Cover the bowl with plastic wrap and place in the refrigerator for at least 2 hours or overnight. The batter is ready when it's firm and doesn't stick on your finger. If the dough still seems sticky after refrigerating, stir in a little more flour.

Heat oven to 350 degrees.

On a heavily floured surface, roll a handful of dough to ⅛-inch thickness, dusting with flour to keep it from sticking to the rolling pin or counter as you rotate the dough. Cut the cookies using a lightly floured 2- or 3-inch round biscuit or cookie cutter, turning the cutter slightly as you lift it off the dough. Slide a lightly floured spatula under each cookie to ease it from the surface and transfer it to a cookie sheet, placing cookies 1 inch apart. Sprinkle a generous amount of sugar onto the tops of the cookies.

Bake 7–8 minutes. The cookies go from white to golden brown in a matter of seconds, so watch closely in the last minute. The whiter the cookies, the softer they are in the middle. For a crisper cookie perfect for coffee dunking, bake 8–10 minutes total, removing from oven as they turn a darker shade of brown.

Transfer to a cooling rack. Let cool completely before stacking cookies in an airtight container, where they will keep nicely for at least 3 weeks.

Repeat in batches with remaining dough.

Jan's Club Cracker Bars

Jan Maguire
Woodbury, MN

the dish

No-bake, sweet-and-salty bars that are quick and easy to make but a dual-texture treat you will want to slowly devour.

the tell

If you've ever had the pleasure of enjoying Christmas crack aka "saltine cracker toffee," these addictive bars will blow your mind.

My friend Nikki's mom, Jan, is known for her Club Cracker bars, which have a scrumptious, sink-your-teeth-into-it texture and chocolatey-caramel flavor. Whenever she brings them to a family gathering or potluck, she gets numerous requests for the recipe.

Like Christmas crack, these bars start with a foundation of crackers lined up in the bottom of a jelly roll pan. But hold the saltines! This recipe calls for buttery Club Crackers, which tells you right there that you are in for a real treat. Add a caramel layer with graham cracker crumbs and shredded coconut mixed in, top it all off with some melted chocolate, and the result is a delightful bar that is both sweet and salty, gooey and crisp for an indulgent eating experience.

It's a recipe Jan began making in the 1980s for all types of occasions, from church functions to card club to family reunions. She appreciates how it's a quick and easy dessert you can pull together in a pinch as long as you have all the ingredients. "Everyone loves these bars," says Jan, who delights in the reaction when people bite into them. "They often say 'ooh' or 'you should try this' because of the unique texture from the cracker combined with caramel."

MAKES ABOUT 5 DOZEN BARS

approximately 40 Club Crackers

1 cup (2 sticks) butter

½ cup milk

2 cups packed brown sugar

2 cups graham cracker crumbs (about 2 sleeves)

2 cups sweetened (or unsweetened) coconut

3 (4.4-ounce) chocolate bars (Hershey)

Line a (10x15–inch) jelly roll pan with Club Crackers face down.

In a large saucepan, melt butter and add milk and brown sugar, stirring to combine. Stir in graham cracker crumbs and coconut and bring to boiling. Boil mixture for 7 minutes, stirring constantly. Remove from heat and spread over crackers.

In a small saucepan set over low heat, melt chocolate. Spread over bars while they are still warm. Refrigerate bars to cool. Cut them as soon as the chocolate has hardened (see tip). Store in the refrigerator or freezer until ready to serve.

tips Jan cuts the bars as the chocolate begins to harden but before they are completely cool, noting, “It’s easier to cut the bars when the caramel layer is not completely cooled.”

She suggests cutting them small and keeping them in the freezer, so they are at the ready when you need a sweet treat.

Make sure the crackers are lined up tightly along the bottom of the pan to create a good foundation for the caramel layer; otherwise, the caramel may seep through and the bars will stick to the pan.

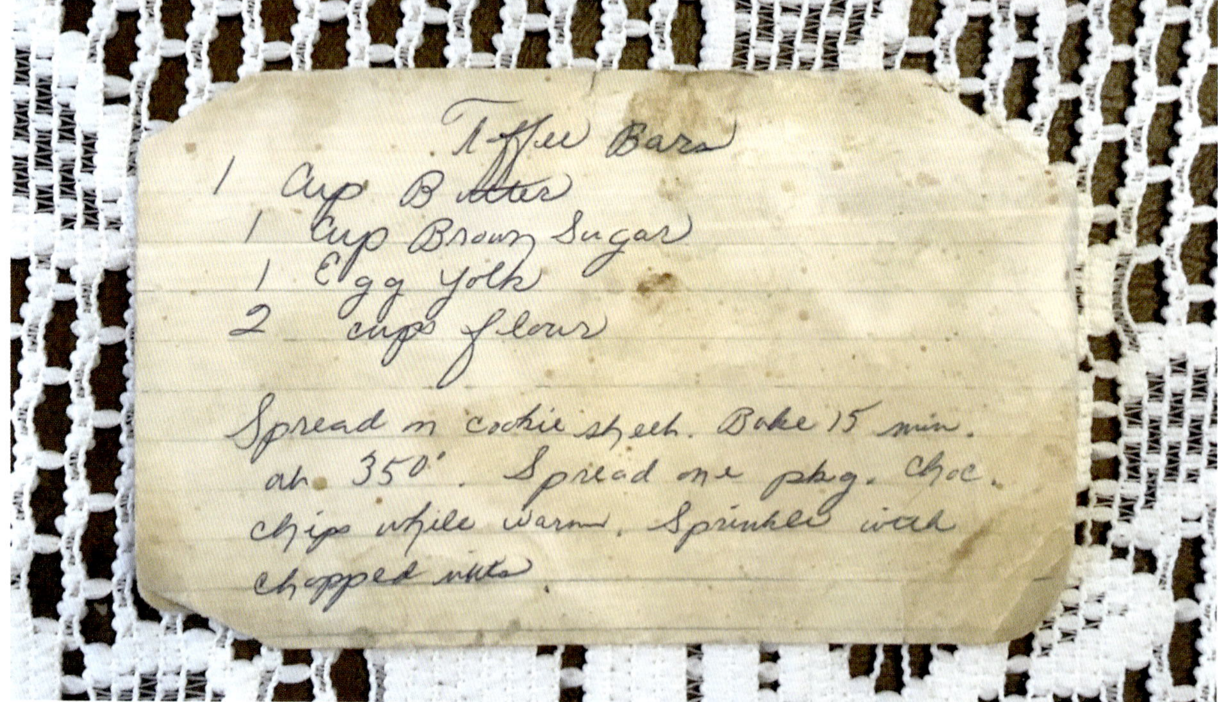

Toffee Bars

1 Cup Butter
1 Cup Brown Sugar
1 Egg Yolk
2 cups flour

Spread on cookie sheet. Bake 15 min. at 350°. Spread one pkg. Choc. chips while warm. Sprinkle with chopped nuts

Toffee Bars

the dish

A go-to recipe for fast and easy bars with a tender, shortbread base topped with chocolate and chopped nuts.

the tell

Growing up, toffee bars were a staple treat my mom made just for us. Unlike other baked items she made, these bars were not meant to serve for company or to give away to others. Cut into perfect squares and placed on a paper plate that was double-wrapped in plastic bags with twist ties, the bars were a welcome sight whenever they appeared in the refrigerator.

My mom likely made these bars so frequently because they require only a few ingredients and can be made lickety-split. First, bake a simple shortbread crust; then the recipe calls for sprinkling chocolate chips across the top, allowing them to melt a little before spreading the chocolate across the pan, and topping with some chopped nuts. This is where I came in.

One of my core memories from childhood is being on standby in the kitchen while my mom baked, eagerly waiting to lick any dish or utensil before it hit the sink or ready to lend a hand if asked. My mom didn't take me up on many offers to help, but she did entrust me with chopping nuts and allowed me to use her seventies vintage nut grinder, which was harvest gold on top and had a glass bottom. I didn't love nuts when I was a kid and thought this was an unnecessary step, but I happily obliged to get that much closer to eating whatever treat was on deck.

Today I love the nuts for the added crunch and touch of pizzazz they give to the finished bars, making them a worthy dessert for a party or a potluck. However, it's also perfectly acceptable to make a batch of toffee bars to keep for yourself to indulge in at your pleasure.

MAKES ABOUT 3 DOZEN BARS

1 cup (2 sticks) butter, at room temperature

1 cup packed brown sugar

1 egg yolk

2 cups flour

1 (12-ounce) package chocolate chips

½ cup chopped walnuts

Heat oven to 350 degrees.

In a large bowl, mix butter, brown sugar, and egg yolk. Add flour and blend well. Spread dough on a 12x17–inch jelly roll pan, pressing down with your fingers. Bake 15 minutes or until golden brown.

While bars are still warm, top with chocolate chips. As the chocolate melts, spread it across the bars. Top with chopped nuts.

tips We always topped the bars with walnuts. Toasting them for a few minutes on the stovetop makes them even more flavorful.

For maximum freshness, store the bars in the refrigerator. The bars will keep for several days.

Thunderstorm Bars

Lamm Sisters
Minneapolis, MN

the dish

Concocted during a Minnesota thunderstorm by two sisters, these deliciously addictive bars include a base of cereal, peanut butter, and peanuts topped with a thick layer of decadent chocolate.

the tell

Sometimes the best recipes strike like a bolt of lightning.

Carrie says her younger sisters came up with their now family-favorite bars one stormy night in the seventies when they were scared and couldn't sleep. It was 1974: Carrie was fourteen years old, her sister Marcia was twelve, and the youngest sister, Liz, was seven.

Liz remembers the occasion well. It was the middle of the night, and she couldn't sleep due to the loud claps of thunder. She started rearranging her bedroom, which awakened her older sister Marcia, who came in to see what was going on. When Liz told her she was scared and couldn't sleep, Marcia offered to stay up with her, and they decided to bake something to take their mind off the storm.

They found their way to the kitchen pantry to scrounge for ingredients to make bars, the perfect comfort food to ride out the storm. Armed with a recipe for Special K bars from a family friend, the sisters had to improvise and substitute a few ingredients, but the new recipe was such a hit that it's been a part of their regular rotation of treats for nearly fifty years. "Ever since we made those bars on that night, we have called them 'Thunderstorm Bars,'" says Liz.

Carrie says the original recipe for Special K bars came from her high school best friend Catherine's mother. Carrie recalls how her friends would often have get-togethers and sleepovers that they called "Reject Parties" because they were more interested in academics, service, and sports over dating. "We would chat, play games, watch *Saturday Night Live*, and sometimes sleep over," says Carrie, who adds that the evening menu typically consisted of pizza, Tab cola, and desserts such as M&M's or "maybe something more exotic like blondies, brownies, etc."

"At one of these parties, Catherine's mom, Joanne, made these bars, and I was hooked. I asked for the recipe, and we began making them at my house. Our family called them 'Catherine's Peanut Bars.'" That is, until her sisters' evening of thunderstorms and hunger desperation, when they had to tweak the recipe based on what they had in the pantry, hence the name.

"This has been a go-to dessert and a part of our family lore since the early seventies," says Carrie, adding that the bars are the one dessert someone brings every time they gather. "Each time I visited my kids at college in Missouri, I brought or made them there. When I went to Chicago for spring break I planned to show up with an entire pan of bars, carefully packed in a carry-on," says Carrie. "You cannot not bring them. They are expected!" ➤➤

recipe for: Thunderstorm Bars
9x13 pan
1/2 c brown sugar
1/2 c light corn syrup
2 T. butter
1/2 c peanut butter
1 1/2 c rice krispies
1/2 c corn flakes
7 oz party peanuts
FROSTING 6T. milk, 6T. butter
1 c. brown sugar, 1 bag semisweet
chocolate chips
serves:

CR10-66

Thunderstorm Bars

MAKES 32 BARS

bars

3 tablespoons butter or margarine

½ cup packed light or dark brown sugar

½ cup light corn syrup

½ cup smooth peanut butter

1 cup peanuts

1 cup cornflakes

1½ cups crispy rice cereal

frosting

5 tablespoons butter or margarine

1 cup packed light or dark brown sugar

6 tablespoons milk or half-and-half

1 (12-ounce) package semisweet chocolate chips

Use a 9x13–inch ungreased pan; line with foil or parchment if desired.

In a large saucepan, melt 3 tablespoons butter, ½ cup brown sugar, and light corn syrup to just about boiling. Be careful not to overheat or the bars will be rock hard.

Remove pan from heat and stir in peanut butter and peanuts, then gently stir in the cereals. Spread mixture into prepared pan. Set aside to cool.

For frosting, in a medium saucepan, melt 5 tablespoons butter and stir in 1 cup brown sugar and milk; heat to just about boiling. This mixture will boil fast; do not leave the stove.

Remove from heat. Add chocolate chips and let them melt on their own, then whisk lightly until smooth. Pour over bars. Refrigerate to set.

tips Buy high-quality chocolate chips if you can. Carrie recommends Ghirardelli.

In a pinch, you can make the bars with all cornflakes and no Rice Krispies.

The bars travel well, even in a cooler in the summer. They also freeze well if you are lucky enough to have any leftovers.

Don't multitask while making the bars or you may end up with hard bars or gritty ganache.

If the frosting is less creamy and more gritty, you overdid the boiling or the whisking; next time take it down a notch.

Carrie's kitchen advice

Read the recipe at least twice before making it.

Bring the recipe (or a picture of it) to the store when shopping for ingredients.

NEVER make anything the first time and serve to company.

Rhubarb Pie Bars

the dish

Rhubarb pie in the form of bars is perfect for picnics, potlucks, and any time you are craving pie. No fork necessary.

the tell

I was inspired to make rhubarb pie bars after years of making apple pie bars, which are essentially pie made in a rimmed baking sheet instead of a pie plate and cut into bars.

I credit my cousin-in-law Becci for introducing me to making pie in bar form, aka slab pie. She'd often bring apple bars (as her family calls them) to the July Fourth Peterson potlucks, where they were always a hit. There is something special about serving pie in cute little squares topped with a drizzle of glaze that makes people go wild and beeline to the dessert table.

Becci's recipe hails from her mom, Linda, who has been making apple bars for more than thirty years; it's one of her signature recipes. Linda recalls being nervous about how they'd go over the first time she brought apple bars to a family reunion, as her own mother was the "pie queen" and skeptical a bar could be as tasty as pie. "Thankfully, she loved them, as well as the rest of the family, so I was 'burdened' with always providing the apple bars," says Linda.

While I make apple bars a few times each fall, I am happy to have a spring counterpart using rhubarb. I simply swap out apples for an equal amount of rhubarb, or sometimes mix it up with a blend of rhubarb and strawberries for a bit more sweetness.

With either the apple or the rhubarb version, it's my favorite way to make and eat pie. There is no need for a fork; you don't need to fuss with whipped topping or ice cream; and the bars are very portable and hold well. It all adds up to a great dessert to bring to a potluck, picnic, or any pie-eating occasion.

There is also some built-in confidence when making slab pie in a sheet pan because you can take comfort in knowing the bars will turn out and be share-worthy. Have you ever made a pie and been nervous to cut into it before serving, afraid of a soggy bottom? Since you cut the bars before serving, you can make sure they are baked through and even do some taste testing. You can't do that with a regular pie! »

➛ Rhubarb Pie Bars

SERVES 20–24

crust

2½ cups flour

1 tablespoon sugar

1 teaspoon salt

1 cup vegetable shortening (Crisco)

1 egg yolk with milk to make ⅔ cup liquid; reserve egg white for egg wash

¾ cup crushed cornflakes

filling

3 cups sliced rhubarb

1½ cups granulated sugar

glaze

1 cup powdered sugar

½ teaspoon vanilla

2–3 tablespoons milk

Heat oven to 400 degrees.

In a large bowl, whisk together flour, 1 tablespoon sugar, and salt. Use a pastry cutter or fork to cut in shortening until crumbly. Stir in egg yolk–milk mixture until dough comes together. Divide into 2 parts. Roll one to fit in a (10x15–inch) jelly roll pan. Sprinkle cornflakes over crust.

Mix filling ingredients and dollop over cereal crumbs. Roll out remaining crust and place over rhubarb. Beat egg white and brush on top of crust. Bake for about 50 minutes or until crust is golden brown.

Make the glaze by mixing powdered sugar with vanilla and milk. Drizzle glaze over bars while they are cooling.

tips You can substitute Frosted Flakes or Wheaties for the cornflakes.

Replace one cup of rhubarb with strawberries for a slightly sweeter bar.

The recipe calls for shortening, and Linda prefers butter-flavored Crisco.

When rolling out the crust, Linda says, “The crust mixture should be on the moist side instead of dry. The less handling the better!”

Rhubarb Meringue Dessert

the dish

A rhubarb dessert with a buttery crust, a luscious custard-like filling, and a cloud of fluffy meringue.

the tell

This old-fashioned rhubarb dessert comes from a tattered magazine clipping I found tucked inside my mom's recipe box. I remember her making it on occasion during rhubarb season, and I was always impressed by the towering fluffy meringue on top.

It's the kind of dessert reserved for Sundays, when there was more time to spend in the kitchen and when we'd visit my grandparents to share a homemade treat. While it does go in and out of the oven three times, the payoff is a scrumptious and pretty dessert that will knock the socks off any rhubarb lover.

When I first attempted this recipe, I'll admit I was a bit intimidated by making meringue. But to my surprise it came together quite easily after I did a little research on how to identify soft and stiff peaks when beating egg whites—essential for achieving that perfect, airy topping (see tips).

SERVES 12–15

crust

1 cup flour

1 tablespoon sugar

1 cup (2 sticks) butter, cold

filling

2 cups sugar

⅓ cup flour

1 teaspoon salt

6 egg yolks, beaten (save whites for meringue)

1 cup heavy cream

5 cups sliced rhubarb

meringue

6 egg whites

½ teaspoon cream of tartar

¾ cup sugar

1 teaspoon vanilla

Heat oven to 350 degrees. Grease a 9x13–inch baking dish; set aside.

For the crust, in a medium bowl combine 1 cup flour and 1 tablespoon sugar. Use a pastry cutter or fork to cut in butter until crumbly. Press into prepared baking dish. Bake for 20 minutes. While crust cools, prepare the filling.

For the filling, in a large bowl combine 2 cups sugar, ⅓ cup flour, and salt, mixing well. Stir in egg yolks and cream, add rhubarb, and pour over crust. Bake for 50–60 minutes or until set.

For the meringue topping, in the bowl of a stand mixer use whisk attachment to beat egg whites and cream of tartar on medium speed until soft peaks form. Gradually beat in ¾ cup sugar, 1 tablespoon at a time, until stiff peaks form. Beat in vanilla.

Spread meringue over hot filling and bake for 12–15 minutes, until golden brown. Cool on a wire rack. Refrigerate for 1–2 hours before serving.

tips for making meringue

Use room-temperature eggs.

Use a glass or stainless steel mixing bowl, free of grease or soap residue.

Use a wire whisk attachment if possible.

Start slow and increase speed as you go.

To check the peak stage, lift the whisk from the mixture:

If the peaks flop over, they're soft.

If they stand straight up, they're stiff.

Frozen Strawberry Dessert

the dish

A simple crumb crust topped with a strawberry ice cream layer and more crumbs.

the tell

A grandma's house is often synonymous with cookies and treats, but my grandma Frances took things up a notch with a standing dessert date with our family each week. Each Sunday afternoon we'd make the short drive from our home in Cloquet, Minnesota, to my grandparents' house in Carlton. This tradition was something I looked forward to—not just to see my grandparents, whom I adored, but to discover what kind of dessert my grandma had whipped up for us that week.

While the guys would retreat to the den to watch sports on TV, my mom and I would sit with my grandma in the living room, flipping through her stash of women's magazines and chatting about the week's events (including the latest celebrity gossip). Eventually we'd all gather in the kitchen, where my grandma would unveil her latest creation—often a sheet pan cake or frozen dessert.

Her strawberry frozen dessert remains one of my favorites. I've always loved the crumbs that form the crust and topping. It's a dish my mom also made on numerous occasions and one I like to make today—particularly in the summer, when an ice cream–like dessert really hits the spot.

Food safety note: This recipe uses raw eggs. For best safety practices, use pasteurized eggs or be aware that consuming raw eggs carries a risk of foodborne illness.

SERVES 12

crust

1 cup flour

½ cup packed brown sugar

½ cup chopped walnuts

½ cup (1 stick) butter, melted

filling

2 egg whites (see note)

1 cup granulated sugar

2 cups strawberries, fresh or frozen, thawed

2 teaspoons lemon juice

1 cup whipped cream

Heat oven to 375 degrees. Mix crust ingredients and spread loosely on a rimmed baking sheet. Bake for 20 minutes, stirring occasionally. Cool slightly.

Meanwhile, prepare the strawberry layer. Using a blender or mixer, blend the egg whites, sugar, strawberries, and lemon juice until mixture fluffs up a bit. Gently fold in the whipped cream.

Pat two-thirds of the baked crumbs in a 9x13–inch pan, a pie plate, or a springform pan. Pour the strawberry mixture on top of the crumb crust. Sprinkle remaining crumbs on top.

Freeze until set, approximately 4 hours.

tips While my grandma and mom made this dessert in a 9x13–inch pan, I like to make it in a pretty pie plate or a springform pan for a deeper and more elegant presentation.

Optional: Garnish with fresh strawberries.

the dish

A dreamy fluff of peanut butter blended with cream cheese and whipped cream that sits atop a graham cracker crust.

Peanut Butter Pie

Sharon True
Cloquet, MN

the tell

This pie, my oh my! Sharon, a lifelong neighbor at my childhood home who swapped many recipes with my mom through the years, introduced me to peanut butter pie.

I adore this recipe for the indulgent combo of peanut butter and cream cheese that alone is completely enchanting, but also folding in whipped topping gives this pie an airiness that is like eating a cloud of peanut butter fluff. Plus this recipe yields two pies, and how can you go wrong with more pie?

I still remember the excitement when the True family moved into the neighborhood. They came from a faraway land (aka Wisconsin) and had two kids close in age to me and my brothers, which meant instant playmates. Our parents hit it off, and our families grew close as neighbors often do, spending much time together. The Trues were present at many milestone moments in our lives, and our families were frequent guests at each other's tables.

It was a fun time to be a kid, as we'd be outside or out of the house for much of the day, biking around the neighborhood or popping in and out of other neighbors' houses. It was thrilling to go inside someone else's house, and the Trues had cable TV and a whole new set of snacks, from Tab soda to Sharon's homemade specialties such as monster cookies or finger Jell-O.

When we celebrated birthdays together, I remember peanut butter pie was a standout dessert Sharon made at the request of her son Todd. "I have never been a big fan of frosting on cake as it's just too sweet for me, but I have always liked peanut butter so that's how it all started," says Todd, who adds that he has attempted to make the pie a couple of times, but "it's always better when it's made by your mom."

Sharon continues to make the special pie each Thanksgiving. And thankfully for Todd, there is always an extra pie for him to take home!

SERVES 12–16

1 (8-ounce) package cream cheese, at room temperature

1 cup peanut butter

1½ cups powdered sugar

1 (16-ounce) container whipped topping (Cool Whip)

2 graham cracker crusts (see note)

chocolate shavings or chocolate chips

In a large bowl, use a hand or stand mixer to blend the cream cheese and peanut butter together. Add powdered sugar and mix well. Fold in whipped topping and divide the mixture between the graham cracker crusts. Sprinkle chocolate shavings or chocolate chips on top. Chill in the refrigerator or freezer until ready to serve.

Sarah's notes

Store-bought crusts work just fine, but it is easy to make your own graham cracker crust. For 1 crust:

> Combine 1½ cups graham cracker crumbs, ¼ cup sugar, and 6 tablespoons melted butter in a bowl, mixing well. Press into a pie plate using your fingers and/or a spoon. Bake at 350 degrees for about 10 minutes. Cool before filling.

To make gluten-free, use gluten-free graham crackers.

Choose your texture: Refrigerating the pie results in a softer, fluffier texture, while freezing the pie gives it a firmer texture that is more like ice cream.

Homemade Chocolate Pudding

Lori Smith
Sioux Falls, SD

the dish

Rich and velvety smooth homemade chocolate pudding.

the tell

There is nothing quite like the taste of rich, homemade chocolate pudding—especially when it carries the warmth of childhood memories. For Lori, this recipe takes her back to making pudding alongside her grandma.

Each Sunday when she was a young girl, Lori and her parents would make a short drive from their home near Big Stone City, South Dakota, to visit her grandparents' house for dinner. Her grandparents owned and operated Dexter's Store, located northwest of Correll, Minnesota. The store occupied the front of the building, while their home was nestled in the back, complete with an abundant garden and a lively mix of chickens.

The tiny yet inviting kitchen stands out in Lori's memories, as it's where she would help Grandma Dexter make chocolate pudding they would eat for dessert after their family meal together. "I remember being impatient but eager to retrieve ingredients to make the pudding so we could eat it sooner," says Lori, who continues to make the beloved pudding for special occasions. "I make it as a special treat and always have fond memories of my grandma."

In addition to the decadent chocolate pudding, Lori's grandma was well known for her homemade peanut brittle. She made and gave away hundreds of pounds each Christmas season, and it has been said that her famous peanut brittle traveled to all fifty states, even Alaska!

Though many years have passed, Lori still stirs up the same chocolate pudding, proving that some recipes, like the best memories, never fade—they only grow sweeter with time.

SERVES 4

2 eggs, well beaten

1 cup sugar

¼ cup cocoa

¼ cup hot water

¼ cup cornstarch

2 cups milk

1 teaspoon vanilla

In a large saucepan, stir together eggs, sugar, and cocoa. Add ¼ cup hot water and stir until smooth. Slowly add cornstarch and stir until smooth. Place saucepan over medium heat and gradually add milk, stirring until mixture thickens, about 5 minutes. Stir in vanilla. Serve immediately.

just for fun

Besides her grandmother, Lori credits her mother as one of her biggest influences in the kitchen: "My mother made many great meals, like baked chicken and rice or pork chops and rice, that I have continued to make, and now my adult daughter also makes those same meals."

the dish

These soft, buttery caramels, individually wrapped in waxed paper, make the sweetest treat to gift to others—even though you'll probably want to keep them all for yourself.

Betty's Caramels

Liz Murphy
St. Paul, MN

the tell

In my St. Paul neighborhood sits a charming vintage shop named after a remarkable woman known for her hospitality, appreciation of the finer things in life, and exquisite baking—especially her legendary caramels. Grandma Betty left a lasting impression on all who knew her, including her granddaughter Liz, who founded the store that carries on her grandma's legacy.

When I first wandered into Betty's Antiques, I was immediately enamored with all the dainty dishes, gorgeous linens, and European-inspired treasures that made it feel like a welcome step back in time. Plus, there happened to be a bowl of the most delicious caramels I ever tasted—a perfect touch to welcome visitors and pay homage to the store's namesake.

Liz explains that Betty was always a welcoming hostess at her home in Le Sueur, Minnesota. Whether it was inviting her grandchildren for a sleepover and an evening watching Lawrence Welk or entertaining her group of lady friends with afternoon cocktails or bridge club, Betty's home was a haven of joy and camaraderie—and treats, lots of treats. "She was an entertainer," says Liz of her grandma, who was a young widow and busy career woman as the director of nurses at the hospital in Le Sueur, "yet she always had time to do a lot of hosting, entertaining, cooking, and baking."

Family visits to Grandma Betty's were synonymous with delicious treats and cherished memories. From mint brownies to popcorn balls wrapped in waxed paper and stored in a paper bag on top of the refrigerator, she always stocked special sweets to have at the ready for Liz, her sister, and their cousins who were frequent guests. Liz recalls how she and her cousins would often end up in the basement where the deep freezer was, and they'd prop up their cousin Casey to crawl in the freezer and get the treats.

Yet the homemade caramels hold a special place in Liz's heart; they were distributed in little cardboard boxes around the holidays, each caramel individually wrapped.

Liz notes that Grandma Betty's caramels can be tricky to make and require patience, attention to detail, and perhaps a dose of humor. One amusing anecdote captured in a family cookbook makes apparent Betty's dedication to her caramels: She enlisted the help of a local handyman, Dick, to save her from a caramel catastrophe. Anyone who has made caramels knows the recipe requires constant stirring for an extended time and the mixture can't be left unattended. One day as Betty was at the stove stirring the caramel, the phone rang. Her daughter Karen was caught off guard when a man answered. Karen thought she had the wrong number, but Betty had instructed Dick, who was helping to paint the dining room that day, to answer the phone and later switched spots with him so she could chat with Karen while he stirred away.

Liz has many memories of special moments visiting her grandma, such as a table set for two for lovingly prepared meals with special touches, including fancy dishes and goblets as well as cloth napkins. Liz learned the art of cherishing the finer things without fear of imperfection, a lesson she now imparts in her shop. "Her things were accessible and ready to use," says Liz, who encourages her customers to live like Betty and not be afraid to use the good dishes. "You don't need to polish the silver. If you are going to have these fancy things in your cupboard, get them out and use them."

In Liz's shop, Grandma Betty's spirit lives on—a reminder to embrace the beauty of the past and create moments of joy and connection. Just as Betty encouraged her loved ones to indulge in life's little pleasures, Liz invites her customers to do the same, reminding them that some things, like caramels, are meant to be enjoyed wholeheartedly, one sweet moment at a time.

Betty's Caramels

MAKES ABOUT 10 DOZEN

2 cups granulated sugar

⅔ cup firmly packed brown sugar

1 (12-ounce) can sweetened condensed milk

2 cups light corn syrup

1 cup (2 sticks) plus 6 tablespoons butter

Prepare a 9x13–inch baking dish or jelly roll pan by greasing it with butter or lining with parchment.

Combine all ingredients in a saucepan set over medium-high heat and cook, stirring constantly. Boil for about 55 minutes or until the mixture registers 243 degrees with a candy thermometer.

Test to see if the caramel is ready by dropping a spoonful in a cup of ice water. If you can mold the caramel with your fingers and it feels firm yet malleable, it's ready.

Pour caramel into prepared pan and cool; refrigerate for several hours or overnight.

Bring caramel to room temperature, then cut into rectangles and wrap in waxed paper.

note Straight from Betty: "Wrap in waxed paper, place in holiday boxes, and distribute to loved ones, who will hide them from their loved ones so they can enjoy them ALL by themselves."

just for fun Liz's family has a darling cookbook featuring all of their Betty favorites. Liz's cousin Megan gathered recipes the cousins remember most, typed them up, and layered in pictures of Betty, her family, and the handwritten versions of some of her recipes. There are also sweet anecdotes and memories of Betty shared by family members.

Kitchen Wisdom

If cookie dough is too soft to roll, chill in the refrigerator.

If cookie dough is too dry, work in 1 tablespoon of butter.

Always bake a test cookie to see if the consistency of the dough is right and to monitor the oven temperature.

When a cake cracks, the temperature may be too high.

A sticky crust means too much sugar or underbaked.

If a cake breaks in the center, there is likely too much flour.

***Favorite Recipes*, from the American Association of University Women/Silver Bay, Minnesota, Branch (1974)**

When cutting marshmallows, dip your scissors in water.

Lightly grease your grater with butter to prevent cheese from sticking to it.

When measuring peanut butter, moisten the measuring cup and it will make it easier to remove.

Use a wet knife to cut a cake for a cleaner cut.

***Love: The Main Ingredient, Welcome to the Banquet*, from the Banquet meal ministry in Sioux Falls, South Dakota (1990)**

A rib of celery in your bread bag will keep the bread fresh for a longer period of time.

To keep chocolate cakes brown on the outside, dust the greased pan with cocoa instead of flour.

Save the circular cardboards from frozen pizzas and cover with foil to transport cakes.

When rolling out sugar cookies, use powdered sugar on your surface instead of flour.

If gravy seems greasy, try adding a small amount of baking powder and the grease should disappear.

When frying meat, sprinkle salt on the bottom of the fry pan to prevent sticking and splashing.

Bacon dipped in flour will not shrink (and also gives the bacon a texture like it was deep-fried!).

***Favorite Recipes II*, from Zion Lutheran Church, Cloquet, Minnesota (1996)**

Treasured Holiday Traditions
Here's what's cookin'
Deviled Ham Cheese Ball 179
Easter Pie 181
Ham Loaf & Mustard Sauce 184
Raisin Sauce (for Ham) 187
Sausage Stuffing 189
Here's what's cookin'
Cheesy Party Potatoes 191
Grandma McMahon's Potato Dressing 192
Cranberry Fluff 194
Carol's Christmas Jell-O 196
Chocolate-Covered Cherry Bars 198
Mother's Sour Cream Cutout Cookies 200
Flamossa with Raspberry Sauce 203
Potica 207
English Holiday Fruitcake 210

It's no surprise that holidays hold many of our most treasured food traditions, marked by people gathering around meals that are lovingly prepared year after year.

As spring approaches I find myself thinking of Easter at my grandparents' house, with vivid memories of a platter of perfectly sliced ham adorned with pineapple and maraschino cherries. It was always accompanied by raisin sauce (my favorite way to eat ham to this day) and my grandma's famous cheesy potatoes. For other families springtime is an occasion to revisit time-honored traditions like making potica (also popular at Christmas) or savory Italian Easter pies filled with peppery eggs and cheese.

While I appreciate Easter and springtime feasts, it's the stretch between Thanksgiving and New Year's Eve that I find to be truly magical. I cannot get enough of the festive decor and twinkly lights against the backdrop of Minnesota's snowy weather that brings on a cozy feeling unlike any other time of year. I also love this period that's steeped in tradition with many of our most beloved foods.

For me, the real fun begins the week of Thanksgiving, when I start prepping dishes for our Turkey Day feast, most notably my mom's sausage stuffing. It's just as much about getting a leg up on the big day as it is about wanting to jump feetfirst into the holiday spirit.

All of the prep and hoopla around Thanksgiving blurs right into holiday baking and several rounds of cookie and lefse making leading up to Christmas. In recent years I've enthusiastically taken on the task of baking many of our family's favorite treats, such as chocolate-covered cherry bars, Nut Goodie bars, and glazed sugar cookies that my mom used to reserve just for this festive time of year. She was known to spend days in the kitchen baking dozens of different cookies, bars, and breads. Then, to the alarm of me and my brothers, she'd give the bulk of it away to friends and neighbors.

For Christmas, we toggle between our Peterson and Granley family celebrations, each with their distinct menu built around ham but with nods to our grandmothers. The Petersons serve ham loaf topped with a rich mustard sauce, a tradition started by my husband Jaye's grandmother Gam. The Granleys opt for a more traditional ham but serve it with a raisin sauce, introduced by my grandma Frances, that gives it a special holiday flair. While our family's ham dishes may differ, both sides share a passion for Scandinavian treats like lefse, krumkake, rosettes, flatbread, and, like just about every other Midwestern family, cheesy potatoes.

New Year's Eve is typically a quieter affair in which we choose to be cozy and comfortable around a fireplace versus fancy and imbibing out on the town. Whenever we can, we like to spend the holiday as a family at Lutsen Ski Resort in northern Minnesota, taking in the fresh air all day on the slopes and snuggling up near the fireplace at night to play cards and board games. We polish off any leftover holiday goodies and indulge in rum cake (see page 140) at midnight. I cherish our time together as a family and love the peacefulness of the night, one last chance to revel in the seasonal sparkles, nosh on some festive treats, and anticipate a fresh start for the new year.

Deviled Ham Cheese Ball

the dish

Devilishly good, this cheese ball is a great appetizer for holiday celebrations and can be divided into smaller portions for a host/hostess gift.

the tell

One telltale sign that a holiday celebration was about to go down at my parents' house: The trusty card table would emerge from storage to take its place in the corner of the dining room. Decorated with a festive tablecloth and napkins, it was the hub for snacks we were allowed to indulge in before the main meal—and likely a smart strategy to keep everyone out of the kitchen so my mom could work in peace.

For our Christmas Eve celebrations the spread included little nibbles like crudités, an olive and pickle tray, and holiday staples such as my mom's party mix and her fancy deviled ham cheese ball, aside a basket of crackers. Adorned with extra pecans and pimento olives, the perfectly round cheese ball was such a thing of beauty that it felt almost criminal to cut into it. But like the perfectly wrapped presents under the tree, its beauty was fleeting: We succumbed to temptation and devoured the cheese ball in its entirety.

True to its name, the recipe includes deviled ham, which comes in a can and is comprised of cured ham and a unique blend of seasonings. This convenient "delicacy" reminds me of Spam, Minnesota's signature canned meat, but deviled ham's ground-up consistency and savory flavorings make it an ideal foundation for delicious dips and spreads. »

tips This recipe needs to be made a few hours before serving but can also be made a few days ahead or even frozen for future use.

This recipe is big enough to make two softball-size cheese balls. I like making one for Christmas and putting the other in the freezer for New Year's Eve.

My mom tops her cheese ball with pimento olives for a festive pop of color.

Give the gift of a cheese ball: Package with fancy crackers, a bottle of wine, or a nice dish and cheese spread knife.

Deviled Ham Cheese Ball

SERVES ABOUT 20

2 (4¼-ounce) cans deviled ham

1 (8-ounce) package cream cheese, at room temperature

1 (8-ounce) package shredded cheddar cheese

2 tablespoons minced onion

1 tablespoon parsley flakes

1 tablespoon lemon juice

1 teaspoon liquid smoke, to taste

½ teaspoon garlic powder

¼ teaspoon celery salt

½ cup chopped nuts (walnuts or pecans)

pecan halves for garnish

Mix together ham, cream cheese, cheddar cheese, minced onion, parsley flakes, lemon juice, liquid smoke (if using), garlic powder, and celery salt. Chill until slightly firm.

Form into 1 large ball or split into 2 smaller balls and set on a serving plate. Roll the cheese ball in chopped nuts to garnish and add pecan halves on top. Cover in plastic wrap and chill for several hours, or store in the freezer.

Easter Pie

Jeannie Passofaro
West St. Paul, MN

the dish

An Italian tradition at Easter that includes tasty half-moon pastry shells with a peppery, cheesy egg filling.

the tell

Easter pies, also known as hethones, are a long-standing tradition in Jeannie's Italian family, dating back to when she grew up on "the Levee" in downtown St. Paul, in an area on the Mississippi River known as "Little Italy" that was home to thousands of Italian immigrants until severe flooding forced them to higher ground in the 1950s.

Jeannie has many fond memories of the close-knit community on the Levee, where she lived alongside multiple generations of her family. She recalls the wood-burning oven her grandpa built in his backyard and how all the women in the neighborhood used it to bake big loaves of bread each weekend. She remembers climbing into a wooden tub with her sister Mary Kay to stomp on grapes her grandpa grew to make wine and having the chance to sample the fruits of their labor. "We'd have the wine on Sundays with dinner. Even my sister and I would get to have some. They'd pour an inch of wine in a glass and fill the rest with 7UP," says Jeannie.

But one of her favorite memories from her time on the Levee was the annual making of hethones, special pies fashioned like calzones but filled with a savory or sweet mixture of eggs, seasonings, and cheeses. Each year Jeannie's grandmas, aunts, and cousins gathered to make the special pies, with everyone having a hand in the process. It was a labor of love that left a lasting impression on Jeannie. "My first memory of making hethones was at my Grandma Daddario's house, right next door to our house on the Levee," says Jeannie. "This was an all-day event, but the time went by fast because of all the fun we had being together."

The recipe for hethones, which Jeannie's family uses to this day, is now a treasured heirloom. It was passed down from her grandmother, who brought it all the way from Casacalenda in the Italian region of Molise. Jeannie notes the hethones, which are large and usually served in slices, were an appetizer or accompaniment to Easter dinner.

Today Jeannie's family continues to gather before Easter to make this special recipe. "We all take part in this wonderful tradition. This day of baking involves all our families, including grandmas, children, grandchildren, cousins, the whole gang," says Jeannie. "The youngest ones make the holes [steam vents] with one of Grandma's thimbles, and the older ones each take turns making a complete hethone."

Jeannie even has her grandma's original thimble, a welcome reminder of the past and her ancestors who first brought this tradition to her family's table. "This is a wonderful recipe for always turning out, not always perfect to look at, but it's the taste that's always perfect," says Jeannie. "This is what fills my heart with the delightful memories of the past." »

Easter Pie

MAKES 6 PIES; EACH PIE SERVES 8 AS AN APPETIZER

crust

6¾ cups flour

2 tablespoons salt

1½ cups vegetable shortening (Crisco)

1½ jumbo eggs (see note; about 3 tablespoons), beaten

1½ jumbo egg whites (see note; about 3 tablespoons; save yolks for egg wash)

¾–1 cup water

filling

2 pounds plus 10 ounces basket cheese (see note), grated, about 5¼ cups

2 pounds plus 12 ounces Romano cheese, grated, about 4 cups

2 pounds plus 12 ounces Parmesan cheese, grated, about 4 cups

2 scant tablespoons finely ground black pepper

2 scant tablespoons baking powder

18 whole jumbo eggs

2½ jumbo egg whites (see note; about 5 tablespoons, save yolks for egg wash)

In the bowl of a stand mixer, combine flour and salt. Use the flat paddle attachment to cut in shortening. Add 1½ eggs and 1½ egg whites and mix until blended. Stop mixer and switch to dough hook. Mix in water a little at a time. Knead until dough is smooth and cleans the bowl.

Portion dough into 6 (approximately 7-ounce) pieces and wrap in plastic wrap. Refrigerate; dough can be made 2–3 days ahead.

To make the filling, in a large bowl combine all ingredients and use hands to mix.

When ready to bake pies, bring dough to room temperature. Heat oven to 350 degrees and lightly flour a baking sheet; set aside. On a floured surface roll each dough portion to about an 11x13–inch oval, approximately ⅛ inch thick. Fold in half, crease, and open flat.

Place a portion of the cheese mixture on the lower half. Pat down to evenly distribute filling, leaving about 1½ inches of dough on the edge. In the top half, use a floured thimble to cut 5 holes, 2 holes on top and 3 closer to the middle. Moisten lower edge of dough with water and fold top half over. Crimp from the edge to the filling. Cut slits in dough edges; moisten pieces and overlap to make "toes."

Transfer hethones to prepared baking sheet. Mix reserved yolks with a little water to thin and smear egg wash on top.

Bake for about 35–40 minutes or until nice and brown. Use a wide spatula or two small ones to remove from baking sheet and place on cooling rack. Place large dish towels or a folded sheet on the table and then place hethones on to completely cool; cover the hethones overnight. The next day, package in plastic bags and freeze or refrigerate.

When ready to eat, bring to room temperature, slice, and enjoy.

just for fun Jeannie says she has long outgrown her recipe box and stores her recipes in three-ring binders: one for sweets, one for everyday recipes, and one for occasional recipes.

Jeannie credits her passion for cooking and baking to her mom, saying, "She taught me so much and encouraged me to have fun in the kitchen."

She says the oldest things in her kitchen are her grandma's thimble, a crimping and cutting tool, a Howdy Doody cookie jar, and herself!

tips **Basket cheese is a fresh, mild Italian cheese traditionally shaped like a basket. It is seasonally available at Italian or ethnic specialty markets leading up to Easter. If you can't find it, substitute queso fresco, which is closest in flavor, or mozzarella—but note that either option will slightly alter the flavor of the filling.**

If there is leftover filling, grease a muffin tin, fill each compartment about half full, and bake at 375 degrees for about 20–25 minutes.

Sarah's notes

To divide an egg in half: crack the egg and whisk it in a bowl. Measure 2 tablespoons for the recipe. To divide an egg white: crack the egg and separate yolk from white. Measure 1 tablespoon of egg white for the recipe. Use remaining egg for something else.

Many family, communal recipes yield large quantities. Jeannie and her family typically prepare multiple rounds of the pie crust and a larger batch of the filling—enough to make about twenty Easter pies to share among their family members or freeze for later use. This version of their family recipe cuts the filling in half but it is still a large quantity. You will likely have extra filling if you want to make more crusts, or use the leftover filling for egg bites (see above).

Ham Loaf & Mustard Sauce

the dish

Flavorful meatloaf made with ground ham and pork, topped with a sweet glaze and accompanied by a side of zingy mustard sauce.

the tell

After Jaye and I married, it was exciting to experience a new set of traditions and fun recipes his family reserved for the holidays. His German grandma, whom the family called Gam, was known for serving ham loaf topped with a rich and creamy mustard sauce.

It sounded a bit peculiar to me and, if I'm being honest, not too appealing. However, after one bite of the juicy meatloaf with the sweet glaze and rich sauce, I was completely won over. Ham loaf and the mandatory mustard sauce have been part of our Christmas (and sometimes Easter) celebrations for the past thirty years.

When Gam passed, I inherited some of her cookbooks and loose recipes. In this small treasure trove, I found Gam's notes from Christmases past, logging every holiday meal she served as well as the guests who were visiting. It was fun to see how ham loaf was a recurring item on a menu that also included broccoli and cheesy potatoes.

Her family remembers one year when Gam was particularly excited to serve ham loaf and overly excited to get everyone's feedback. They said it was the best ham loaf ever and that she'd really outdone herself. Gam, who was known for her mischievous personality, giggled and then admitted that she had forgone making the ham loaf from scratch that year and instead purchased one from Ingebretsen's, the iconic Scandinavian marketplace in Minneapolis.

Thankfully, Gam wasn't too upset about the kudos for her store-bought ham loaf. It's a good lesson that it's perfectly acceptable to let others do the heavy lifting at times if it helps to ease the process of keeping up traditions.

Today we may occasionally purchase a ham loaf at the holidays, but we always make Gam's mustard sauce from scratch. When I make the ham loaf, I have adapted Gam's recipe with a few tweaks to bring it a little closer to the one at Ingebretsen's and—bonus—it's easy to make gluten-free. »

Betty Crocker
Holidays
Thursday - Christmas
Hot cider
Dinner
Roast beef & pork
Mashed potatoes
Gravy
Holiday Treats and Season's Greetings
Christmas Day
cheese/crackers
herring
vegies/dip
Hot cider
Ham loaf
Mustard sauce
party potatoes or chive
mixed vegies
cranberry salad
cottage cheese
pickles/olives
sweet bread/rolls
cookies/ice cream
coffee/milk

Ham Loaf & Mustard Sauce

MAKES 1 LARGE LOAF; SERVES 10–12

glaze

1 cup packed brown sugar

¼ cup apple cider vinegar

1 tablespoon dry mustard

ham loaf

2 pounds ground ham

1½ pounds ground pork

1 cup crushed crackers (see tip)

1 cup evaporated milk

2 eggs, lightly beaten

¼ teaspoon salt

¼ teaspoon pepper

mustard sauce

1 cup half-and-half

1 egg, lightly beaten

¼ cup white vinegar

¼ cup water

¾ cup granulated sugar

2 tablespoons dry mustard

1 tablespoon cornstarch

¼ teaspoon salt

Heat oven to 350 degrees. Lightly grease a 5x9–inch loaf pan. In a small bowl, stir together brown sugar, apple cider vinegar, and 1 tablespoon dry mustard to make a glaze; set aside.

Mix together ham loaf ingredients, form into a loaf, and place in prepared pan. Bake for 1 hour. Spoon glaze over top, then return loaf to oven and bake 30 minutes or until meat thermometer reads 160 degrees.

For the mustard sauce, in a medium bowl combine half-and-half, egg, white vinegar, and water; set aside. In a large saucepan combine granulated sugar, 2 tablespoons dry mustard, cornstarch, and salt; gradually add liquid ingredients. Stir over medium heat until mixture comes to a boil and thickens slightly. Serve immediately with ham loaf; or cool and store, then warm when ready to serve.

tips The hardest part of this recipe (and it isn't that difficult) is sourcing ground ham. You can ask your butcher to grind the ham or visit a specialty meat market.

To make gluten-free, use gluten-free saltine crackers.

Don't skip the mustard sauce: It's what makes this dish unique!

Raisin Sauce (for Ham)

the dish

A sweet and slightly tangy sauce with plump raisins to add some pizzazz to your holiday ham.

the tell

I always thought plain old ham was plain old boring—until I was introduced to Grandma Frances's raisin sauce. If there was ham on her table, there would also be a beautiful gravy boat featuring this sauce, and it remains the only way I can eat plain ham to this day.

Made from common pantry staples, raisin sauce is an easy accompaniment to dress up ham and helps to counter the meat's salty flavor with a bit of sweetness and tang. Plus it gives you a chance to use a pretty gravy boat.

My grandma's ham with raisin sauce remains one of the most memorable meals I enjoyed around my grandparents' dining room table, which was reserved for holidays or special occasions. I'd help her set the table with her elaborate collection of Franciscan Desert Rose china, and she'd remind me how she and her neighbors all bought the same pattern so they could share extra serving pieces when they had showers or big celebrations.

Beyond the ham with raisin sauce, no meal at that table was complete without my grandma's special cheesy potatoes, dressed up with a crunchy topping of crushed sour cream and onion–flavored potato chips (see page 191). And, of course, one of her famous frozen desserts always made an appearance to round out the feast.

MAKES ABOUT 2½ CUPS

½ cup packed brown sugar

2 tablespoons cornstarch

1 teaspoon dry mustard

⅛ teaspoon cloves

1½ cups water

½ cup raisins

2 tablespoons white vinegar

¼ teaspoon grated lemon peel

2 tablespoons lemon juice

2 tablespoons butter

In a large saucepan, combine brown sugar, cornstarch, dry mustard, and cloves, then stir in water, raisins, vinegar, lemon peel, and lemon juice until blended. Set pan over medium-high heat and bring mixture to a boil; cook and stir for 2 minutes, until bubbly and thickened. Stir in butter until melted. Serve warm over ham.

Sausage Stuffing

the dish

My mom makes Thanksgiving stuffing by adding ground sausage and sautéed vegetables to packaged stuffing mix before baking it in foil packets for perfect, crispy edges.

the tell

Families are particular about their stuffing (or dressing), and for good reason. For many of us, myself included, it's the Thanksgiving dish we most look forward to because it's the only time of year we eat it—which means it's best to not mess with tradition!

The recipe for our family's favorite stuffing came from a magazine decades ago, but I credit my mom's added touches for making it a memorable staple of our Thanksgiving table. Like many great home cooks, my mom, Carol, swears by specific brands when making her signature recipes. For her stuffing, she prefers Jimmy Dean bulk sausage. She also only uses Pepperidge Farm Herb Seasoned Classic Stuffing because she fondly recalls her cousin Arlene using this very product as the base for her stuffing, which was always a hit. Carol's other secrets to sausage stuffing success include adding a little grated carrot for some color and baking it in lightly greased foil packets to achieve an optimal texture. No one wants a soggy stuffing! Setting the foil packets atop a sheet pan to pop in the oven results in a just-right texture that is softer in the middle with perfectly crispy edges.

This recipe can be made one or two days in advance, which is helpful for any Thanksgiving host who has to juggle the preparation of multiple dishes. While we wait until just before serving to bake the stuffing, it is nice to have it all prepped and ready to go so there is one less thing to worry about on the day of the feast.

SERVES 20

½ cup (1 stick) butter

2 cups chopped celery

2 cups chopped onion

1 cup grated carrot

1 pound bulk pork sausage

1 (12-ounce) package seasoned stuffing, crushed

1 (14.5-ounce) can chicken broth

¾ cup water

Heat oven to 325 degrees. Lightly grease 3 to 4 (12x15–inch) pieces of foil for the packets; set aside.

In a skillet set over medium-high heat, melt butter and add celery, onions, and carrot. Cook, stirring often, until tender; transfer to a large bowl and set aside.

Brown the sausage; add to the bowl with the vegetables and mix in the stuffing. Add broth and water; toss to mix.

Portion stuffing onto prepared foil and fold edges to seal. Place packets on sheet pan and bake for 45 minutes, opening up the foil packets for the last 10 minutes to allow stuffing to brown and crisp.

tip This recipe can be made gluten-free: Try Aleia's Gluten-Free Savory Stuffing Mix.

Cheesy Party Potatoes

the dish

A tasty mash-up of a trifecta of family recipes for the ultimate cheesy potatoes topped with potato chips.

the tell

Many Midwestern families have some version of cheesy potatoes made with a combination of hash browns, layers of cheese, a can of cream of chicken soup, sour cream, and, if you're lucky, a crispy topping that's typically made from butter-laden cornflakes. It's the dish that shows up at the holidays and potlucks but is also known for its presence in church basements following the death of a loved one, earning it the moniker of "funeral potatoes."

Whatever the occasion, cheesy potatoes is a very rich and indulgent dish, the perfect choice for a celebratory meal or when you need a people-pleasing comfort food. Our family tends to have them twice a year, at Christmas and Easter, usually served alongside ham.

This version is a mash-up of three different recipes served at our family table through the years. The foundation is my mom's recipe, which she remembers clipping from a magazine decades ago: Kemps Dreamy Sour Creamy Potatoes. However, instead of traditional hash browns, I took a cue from my mother-in-law Mary Lou's recipe for Party Potatoes, which uses O'Brien hash brown potatoes that come complete with onions and red and green peppers—adding a little color to the final dish and, bonus, it doesn't require chopping onions, something I try to avoid at all costs.

But hold the applause, as the true icing on the casserole is the crunchy topping, which I credit to my grandma Frances. She was known to top her cheesy potatoes with a layer of sour cream and onion–flavored potato chips. It's the tastiest of toppers that ensures this trifecta of cheesy goodness, representing the best of three family recipes, will be a staple on our holiday table for years to come.

SERVES 10–12

topping

2 cups crushed sour cream and onion–flavored potato chips

4 tablespoons butter, melted

potatoes

1 (28-ounce) package O'Brien hash browns, thawed

1 (12-ounce) container sour cream

½ cup (1 stick) butter, melted

1 (10.5-ounce) can cream of chicken soup

2 cups shredded cheddar cheese

1 teaspoon salt

1 teaspoon pepper

Heat oven to 350 degrees. Grease a 9x13–inch casserole dish. In a medium bowl, combine crushed potato chips and 4 tablespoons melted butter, stirring to mix. Set aside.

In a large bowl, stir together thawed hash browns, sour cream, ½ cup melted butter, cream of chicken soup, cheese, salt, and pepper. Place mixture in prepared dish. Cover with foil and bake for 40 minutes. Remove from oven, remove foil, and add potato chip topping. Return to oven and bake, uncovered, for approximately 10 minutes, until golden brown.

Grandma McMahon's Potato Dressing

Mary Kay Fitzgerald
Woodbury, MN

the dish

A rich mashed potato dressing made in two steps: first boiled and mashed, then slow-roasted for a smooth and silky, velvety texture.

the tell

A keepsake family recipe got a new lease on life when Mary Kay set out to make one of her Grandma McMahon's signature dishes: potato dressing. This unique recipe, made every Thanksgiving by Mary Kay's Irish grandmother, stands apart from traditional mashed potatoes. Sweet onions, a bit of flour, and slow roasting create a dense yet creamy texture with a savory, rich flavor. It's made to feed a crowd: The original recipe called for a whopping twenty pounds of potatoes, half russets, half Yukon golds.

Mary Kay shares that her grandmother was widowed at a young age and left to raise seven children during hard times. She relied on simple, hearty meals to keep the family nourished. It was the end of World War I, during the flu pandemic and on the cusp of the Great Depression. Jobs were scarce, and food was both limited and costly. "People got creative about conserving and cooking frugally," Mary Kay says. "They used inexpensive starches to stretch stews, soups, and one-dish meals like casseroles."

Though Grandma McMahon never wrote down her recipes, she passed on the tradition to her son Eddie, who faithfully prepared the potato dressing each Thanksgiving. Eventually he shared the recipe with the rest of the family. Today Mary Kay's cousins (Eddie's children), their children, and their grandchildren all take part in preserving this treasured dish.

While Mary Kay hadn't made the potatoes herself, she tapped the others in the family who had kept the tradition alive and gave it a go. "While putting it together, I kept thinking, this is just mashed potatoes, but when it was finished and I ate it, I liked it and could taste the difference," says Mary Kay, who notes that the amount of butter, the flour, the onion, and the roasting process give the dish its signature flavor and hearty, satisfying texture.

Mary Kay has since made the dish again, bringing it to her family's annual St. Patrick's Day gathering, when the McMahon clan reunites to march in St. Paul's parade and celebrate their Irish roots. The day involves a meal full of family favorites and Irish fare—now including Grandma McMahon's iconic potato dressing. In serving this dish, Mary Kay not only revived a treasured recipe but also brought Grandma McMahon's presence back to the table.

SERVES 20–25

5 pounds Russet potatoes

5 pounds Yukon gold potatoes

6 tablespoons butter, melted

3–4 medium sweet yellow onions, peeled and chopped

2–2½ cups flour

Peel potatoes and boil until fork tender, about 30 minutes. Drain and mash. Add butter and mix thoroughly.

Heat oven to 325 degrees. Grease a large roasting pan. Add potatoes to pan and stir in onions. Add flour 1 cup at a time, stirring well after each addition until mixed thoroughly. The consistency should be thicker than mashed potatoes but not too doughy. Cover roasting pan with foil and bake for 4–5 hours, stirring every hour.

tips

Mary Kay likes to use Kerrygold butter out of respect for her family's heritage and to make the dish a bit more Irish.

It's easy to halve or quarter this recipe. Mary Kay quartered the original recipe to five pounds of potatoes total for her family of four and reports that it was still a large amount.

This dish can be made ahead of time and then reheated with broth or gravy.

just for fun

Mary Kay is the proud keeper of her mother's Noritake china and silver and has fond memories of a set of Franciscan Apple dishes that her sister has. She also remembers an old crockery pot used for whipping cream, and how her grandmother would grind ham or baloney using a handheld steel meat grinder, then mix in sweet pickles and mayonnaise to make a beloved sandwich spread.

To make your potatoes look extra fancy, use cake decorating tools to pipe a pretty pattern on top.

Cranberry Fluff

Schumann Family,
St. Paul, MN

the dish

Cranberry fluff blends ground cranberries with whipped cream, marshmallows, and crushed pineapple for a dreamy concoction that's light and refreshing and perfect for the holidays.

the tell

When I was searching for a festive fluff to add to my Thanksgiving table, I was thankful that Jason and Kim were so gracious in sharing their family's recipe for cranberry fluff. Jason's grandma Joyce first brought this dish to the table years ago, and it is now a mainstay holiday tradition in their family, carried on by Jason and Kim's grown sons. "It's like a big hug from *and* for family," says Jason. "The sugar rush is a hit for the kids, but it's also a great way to add a layer of sweetness to the traditional turkey, stuffing, ham, and potatoes holiday menu. The color helps add a touch of celebration to the table."

The original recipe appeared in a church cookbook from Kim and Jason's hometown of Starbuck, Minnesota, where they were high school sweethearts.

Jason received a copy of the cookbook from Kim in 1994 when they were in college. Their families and many others in the community grew up with this cookbook in their households, and Jason fondly recalls making many recipes from its pages with his grandma and mom in their kitchens.

Jason remembers making cranberry fluff with his grandma—with one big difference from today. They used to grind up the cranberries with an old metal grinder attached to the table's edge. Jason would hold the bowl and loved the smell of the cranberries all ground up. "It was a fun, interactive way for us to get involved—thus probably why this recipe has extra-special meaning for me."

Today Jason's family uses a food processor for chopping the cranberries, and his sons Brennan and Reed have taken the reins to make it for Thanksgiving and Christmas. "It's fun for them to see the reaction it gets from the family at the meal. It's really the star—especially for leftovers," says Jason.

SERVES 16–20

1 (16-ounce) package cranberries, ground or chopped fine

1½ cups sugar

1 (10-ounce) bag miniature marshmallows

1 (20-ounce) can crushed pineapple, drained

1 (8-ounce) container whipped topping (Cool Whip)

In a large bowl, mix ground cranberries, sugar, marshmallows, and pineapple. Fold in whipped topping and chill overnight.

tips This recipe needs time to chill. Jason typically makes it the night before he plans to serve it.

Adding nuts, common in many fluff recipes, is optional. The Schumanns skip the nuts due to a family member's allergy.

The original recipe called for more sugar (an extra half cup), but Jason assures it won't be missed.

Colored marshmallows are fun to use, especially if you make this dish for Easter, as they look like dyed eggs.

just for fun Always have a freshly baked treat on hand as you never know who's going to stop by. Jason doesn't consistently live by this advice today, but he appreciates how it may have been more relevant in his family's farming days, when neighbors would visit or farmers would come in from the field for a coffee break.

While he uses butter, Jason says his mom remains dedicated to using margarine for many recipes: She claims it tastes better and bakes better.

Carol's Christmas Jell-O

the dish

A delightful dessert for any holiday or celebration, this Jell-O mold includes alternating layers of red and green Jell-O and two layers with sour cream mixed in for a creamy richness.

the tell

We all have special treats or holiday dishes that remind us of gatherings at Grandma's house. For my kids and their cousins, I am sure it will be their grandma Carol's Christmas Jell-O. She made this festive Jell-O mold each year for our family Christmas, and it always brought a smile to the faces of those gathered around the table—not to mention some oohs and aahs.

Featuring alternating layers of red and green Jell-O, including two layers with sour cream mixed in, this is no plain Jane Jell-O. The sour cream gives it a creamy richness in addition to creating the muted red and green layers that make it a visual stunner. Plus, I challenge anyone, kids and adults alike, to resist the fun in slurping up a spoonful of Jell-O.

Some may consider Jell-O to be more of a dessert, but we always serve it as a side dish during our holiday meal, and why not? There are so many other treats to be had for dessert at Christmas. Plus, it's nice to have something light and sweet with our holiday dinner, and it brings a colorful, playful vibe to the table.

For the past several years I have taken on the tradition of making the Christmas Jell-O. There is nothing more exciting than that moment, the big reveal, when it comes time to remove the Jell-O from the mold. I still get nervous that the layers won't adhere or will blend together. However, after some trials and tribulations, I finally have the confidence to keep up this essential family tradition.

tip Our favorite mold: Carol got me hooked on the Tupperware Jel-Ring Jell-O Mold, and it has never let us down. I have other vintage metal molds, but they can be finicky when it comes to the unmolding process. I love this mold because it is just the right size for the Christmas Jell-O, it has a lid for easy transport, and the plastic insert is instrumental to the unmolding process.

SERVES 8–10

2 (3-ounce) packages lime Jell-O

5 cups boiling water, divided

⅔ cup sour cream, divided

2 (3-ounce) packages cherry, raspberry, or strawberry Jell-O

Lightly grease a Jello-O mold (see tip at right).

In a medium bowl, dissolve green Jell-O in 2½ cups boiling water. Pour 1½ cups of mixture into the prepared Jell-O mold (reserve the remaining cup) and chill until set but not quite firm, about 30–45 minutes.

While the first layer is setting in the mold, mix the remaining green Jell-O with ⅓ cup sour cream; set aside.

Once the first layer in the mold has set, carefully spoon the green/sour cream Jell-O over the first layer. Return the mold to the refrigerator and chill until set but not firm, about 30 minutes.

While the first two green layers are chilling, prepare the red layers. In a medium bowl, dissolve red Jell-O in 2½ cups boiling water. Reserve 1½ cups for the third layer of the Jell-O mold; cool on the counter.

Mix the remaining red Jell-O with the remaining ⅓ cup sour cream. Set aside.

When the second layer in the mold is set, gently spoon the plain red layer over the mold. Return the mold to the refrigerator and chill again until set, about 15–20 minutes.

When the third layer is set, gently spoon the last layer, the red Jell-O with sour cream blended in, over the mold. Return to the refrigerator and chill for at least 4–6 hours or overnight.

tips

BEFORE YOU START: Spray the inside of the mold with some PAM or nonstick cooking spray, but blot it with a paper towel so there is just a very thin layer remaining before you start adding in the Jell-O layers. This process will greatly help with sliding the Jell-O out of the mold when it is time to put it on a pretty platter.

LAYERING: If the Jell-O is too firm, the layers won't adhere and may slip apart when unmolded. If the mixture is too warm, it will soften the layer beneath and the layers may run together. Therefore, after the first layer, the Jell-O should be cooled to about room temperature before spooning it onto the mold mixture. In the *Joys of Jell-O*, published by General Foods Kitchens (the original makers of Jell-O), the experts say to chill each layer in the mold until "set but not firm," described as when Jell-O sticks to your finger when touched and/or moves to the side when tilted.

LEVEL UP: While building the layers, place the mold on a baking sheet to make it easier to move the mold in and out of the fridge. Also, ensure you are chilling the mold on a level shelf or you will end up with uneven layers.

BEHOLD THE MOLD: When the Jell-O mold is firm, dip a knife in warm water and run the tip of it around the top edge of the mold to loosen, or moisten the tips of your fingers and gently pull the Jell-O from the top edge of the mold. If you are using the Tupperware Jell-O mold (see page 196): 1) remove the plastic lid, 2) put a moistened serving plate or cake stand over the mold and flip it over so the mold is right side up, 3) carefully and slowly remove the plastic insert (you should see the unmolding magic start to happen before your very eyes), and 4) cue the drumroll when you carefully and slowly lift the plastic mold away for the big reveal.

Chocolate-Covered Cherry Bars

the dish

Festive bars, perfect for the holidays, with a combo of chocolate with creamy fondant, chocolate glaze, and a cherry on top.

the tell

For me, Christmas wouldn't be complete without these bars. Though my family has many special treats we reserve for the most joyous time of year, my mom's chocolate-covered cherry bars rise to the top of my holiday baking bucket list.

These bars were a favorite of my dad's as well, making them more meaningful. He loved Christmas, particularly all the extra goodies my mom would make to share with family and friends. Along with being an enthusiastic taste taster, he took pride in helping to decorate the house. One of his main tasks was to string popcorn and cranberries to hang on the tree. It was a tedious process that took days, but my mom made it worth his while, rewarding him with his favorite treats, including these bars.

Not only are chocolate-covered cherry bars delicious, they also add a pop of color to any dessert tray. The combo of the chocolate layer with the creamy fondant and the chocolate glaze and cherry on top is just the best.

My mom recalls getting the recipe in a small booklet she picked up at the grocery store years ago. But that little recipe made a big impression and has been part of her holiday baking for more than thirty years. It's a straightforward and quick recipe that's great to bring to a holiday party or to share with others. If you do plan to give these bars away, I suggest making a double batch so you can keep some for yourself.

MAKES 3 DOZEN BARS

bars

½ cup (1 stick) butter, at room temperature

½ cup granulated sugar

2 tablespoons cocoa

1¼ cups flour

fondant

2 tablespoons butter, at room temperature

2 cups powdered sugar

2 tablespoons milk

½ teaspoon vanilla

topping

36 maraschino cherries, drained and dried well

1 square unsweetened baking chocolate (or 3 tablespoons cocoa combined with 1 tablespoon shortening)

1 tablespoon butter

Heat oven to 350 degrees.

In a large bowl, combine ½ cup butter, granulated sugar, and cocoa. Mix in flour until crumbly. Press into bottom of an 8x8– or 9x9–inch pan. Bake for 15 minutes. Set aside to cool.

For fondant, in a large bowl combine 2 tablespoons butter, powdered sugar, milk, and vanilla, mixing well. Spread fondant over cooled bars. Add cherries on top of fondant, making 6 rows of 6 cherries.

To prepare glaze, in a small saucepan over low heat melt unsweetened chocolate and 1 tablespoon butter. Drizzle on top of cherries.

Mother's Sour Cream Cutout Cookies

Catherine Walter
St. Paul, MN

the dish

A nostalgic twist on classic cutout cookies—made with sour cream for a slight tang and a sugar-dusted bottom for a hint of sparkle.

the tell

These sour cream sugar cookies have been a time-honored tradition in Catherine's family for generations. The original recipe, dating back to her great-grandmother, has been lovingly passed down—baked by Catherine's grandmother, mother, and siblings and now by her children, grandchildren, and extended family. "I think the sour cream gives the cookies a unique tang that most recipes don't have," says Catherine. "When I serve them, people often ask what I put in the cookie dough."

When her grandmother made the recipe, she rolled the dough into balls and coated them in a cinnamon-sugar mixture before flattening them with the bottom of a water glass. Catherine's mother, however, introduced a new tradition: cutting the dough into festive shapes, sprinkling them with sugar before baking, and frosting the underside, giving both sides a sweet finish. Today Catherine embraces both methods, sometimes keeping it simple with a sprinkle of sugar, and other times decorating with buttercream or royal icing.

The original recipe calls for lard, which Catherine says her mom used when she lived on a farm. However, in later years she switched to Crisco, which the family continues to use today. For Catherine, these cookies are a cherished connection to her mother, who would bake two to four batches—about seventy cookies each—during the holidays. Decorating them was always her mom's favorite part and is something Catherine also looks forward to each year.

Like her mother and grandmother, Catherine takes deep pride in preserving the recipe. Whenever a community or church cookbook asked for submissions, Catherine's mother shared this treasured recipe, and now Catherine herself likes to hand off the recipe whenever she can, spreading the joy of these cookies far beyond her family table. ➤➤

Mother's Sour Cream Cutout Cookies

MAKES ABOUT 6 DOZEN

2 eggs

1 cup vegetable shortening (Crisco)

2 teaspoons baking soda

1 cup sour cream

1 teaspoon vanilla

2 cups sugar, plus more for sprinkling

4½ cups flour, plus more for dusting

Heat oven to 375 degrees.

Mix ingredients in order given, adding enough flour to roll out and cut out cookies with cookie cutters. Transfer cookies to baking sheet and sprinkle sugar on top. Bake for 8–10 minutes.

After cookies have cooled, frost the bottoms of the cookies (see Sarah's note at right).

Sarah's note

Here is our family's favorite glaze for decorating cookies: In a mixing bowl, combine 3 cups powdered sugar with 2 tablespoons light corn syrup and about 2–3 tablespoons milk, adding just enough to reach a consistency similar to Elmer's glue. Divide into separate bowls and tint with food coloring as desired. Spread over cookies. The glaze will harden with a glossy finish. This makes enough glaze for about 4 dozen cookies.

just for fun

Catherine says her parents always made the holidays special. For Christmas her mom baked date bread and something she called a Swedish tea ring. It was a sweet dough, similar to cinnamon rolls, but left whole instead of sliced. She shaped it into an oval on a baking sheet, then cut angled slits partially through the dough. After it rose and baked, she spread strawberry jam into the slits and drizzled the rest with powdered sugar icing. "We always had it with hot chocolate on Christmas Eve after we came home from candlelight services at church."

For Easter her mom made a colorful bunny cake from a white cake mix. She divided the batter into small bowls, tinted each one a different pastel color—pink, purple, yellow—then spooned the colors into two 8-inch round pans, swirling them gently with a knife. Once cooled, she split each cake in half to create two bunnies, frosted them with fluffy white seven-minute icing, and sprinkled them with coconut. A slice was cut out to form the head, with two paper ears tucked in, and the removed piece became the tail. The finishing touches? Pink jelly bean eyes and a bed of green-tinted coconut "grass" with extra jelly beans scattered around. Every grandchild was amazed when she cut into the cake—and now they make it too!

Flamossa with Raspberry Sauce

Barb Pletcher
Woodbury, MN

the dish

Flamossa is a light and airy make-ahead dessert that resembles a meringue-like pudding and is best served topped with raspberry puree and a dollop of whipped cream.

the tell

Many families cap off their holiday meal with festive treats or a dessert they reserve just for this special time of year. Barb and her loved ones look forward to a dessert of Danish origins called flamossa, which has been in their family for decades.

The recipe came from Barb's grandma Hansina, who immigrated from Denmark in 1892 and who referred to flamossa as a "fluff pudding." Made with egg yolks, sugar, gelatin, lemon, and folded-in egg whites, the dessert is light and airy with a unique texture that is not quite a pudding and not quite meringue, making "fluff pudding" a spot-on description.

Hansina, who garnished the flamossa with raspberry sauce and whipped cream, passed on the tradition of making the dessert at Christmas to Barb's mom, Stella, who in turn passed it on to Barb. Today Barb continues to make flamossa each Christmas, to the delight of her husband and their two sons' families. "It's a very light dessert, perfect after a heavy meal, so if you are stuffed and don't feel like a piece of pie, you might still eat this," says Barb, who makes the dessert a day ahead on Christmas Eve. "I always thought it was special, and I am not sure why. I think it's special now because it's a little tricky to make."

I visited Barb to make flamossa with her and her daughter-in-law Jorie, who was eager to learn the family recipe. Barb walked Jorie through each step, particularly those that require a little more attention to detail, like separating the eggs to ensure there is no yolk in the whites or dissolving the gelatin without letting it harden. While it's not an overly complicated recipe, making flamossa takes some patience and concentration.

When preparing flamossa for Christmas, Barb prefers to work alone so she can focus on each step and give the recipe the attention needed to turn out the dessert so loved by her family. The proof is in the (fluff) pudding! »

Flamossa with Raspberry Sauce

SERVES 6–8

flamossa

5 eggs (see note)

1 envelope unflavored gelatin

¼ cup cold water

¼ cup boiling water

¾ cup plus 2 tablespoons sugar

⅛ teaspoon salt

zest and ⅓ cup juice from 1–2 lemons

raspberry sauce

1 (12-ounce) package frozen raspberries, thawed

¼ cup sugar

2 tablespoons cornstarch

whipped cream

1 cup heavy cream

2 tablespoons powdered sugar

splash vanilla

Separate eggs carefully so there's no yolk in the egg whites. Set whites aside.

In a small bowl, soak gelatin in ¼ cup cold water; let stand 5 minutes. Add ¼ cup boiling water and stir. It should not harden.

In the bowl of a stand mixer, beat egg yolks on high; add ¾ cup sugar and salt and beat until light in color. Add gelatin and beat to combine. Add lemon zest and juice and beat to combine. Refrigerate mixture.

In a separate mixing bowl, beat egg whites until peaks flop. Add 2 tablespoons sugar and beat until stiff and glossy, with peaks that stand alone. Fold the egg white mixture into the egg yolk–lemon mixture. Put in serving bowl and refrigerate overnight.

For the sauce, drain raspberries to yield ½ cup of juice; if necessary, add water to equal ½ cup. Set berries aside. In a medium saucepan combine juice with ¼ cup sugar and cornstarch and cook, stirring, over medium heat until mixture thickens. Remove from heat and add in raspberries. Cool and refrigerate until ready to serve.

In a medium bowl, whip heavy cream until it starts to thicken, sprinkle in powdered sugar, and add vanilla. Beat to desired consistency.

Serve flamossa with raspberry sauce and whipped cream.

Food safety note: This recipe uses raw eggs. For best safety practices, use pasteurized eggs or be aware that consuming raw eggs carries a risk of foodborne illness.

tips Have extra eggs on hand in case you make a mistake when separating the yolks from the whites. You don't want any yolks in the whites. You can salvage any mistakes to make scrambled eggs later.

Barb uses her stand mixer for the recipe. She says a hand mixer may make it challenging to beat the eggs to the right consistency.

There are two phases to beating eggs: first the yolks and then the whites. Barb uses the same mixing bowl but washes it in between. She suggests pouring the egg yolk–lemon mixture into a separate bowl and storing it in the refrigerator while beating the egg whites.

Potica

Debbie Vidmar
Chisholm, MN

the dish

A Slovenian sweet bread often made at the holidays featuring layers upon layers of thin pastry with walnut streusel tucked inside.

the tell

Potica is a traditional holiday pastry that, if you know, you know. Perhaps you are lucky enough to be part of a family that made it, or maybe you know someone who makes it. Potica is not something you decide to make on a whim. It takes patience, helps to have a partner, and can't hurt to have a bona fide potica-making expert in your corner. That's why I was tickled to meet Debbie, who was probably born with a taste for potica considering she grew up on the Iron Range—home to a large population of immigrants from Slovenia, where potica originated.

Debbie's passion for potica extends far beyond eating the delicious sweet bread she enjoys "in the morning with butter and at lunch with ham." She takes great pride in the time-honored process that started in her family with her Slovenian grandmother, was honed through the years by her mother, and is carried on today by Debbie and her husband, Greg, as well as other family members who have been eager to learn and maintain this important tradition.

Debbie, who grew up and currently lives in Chisholm, Minnesota, recalls her mother, Sylvia, teaching community education classes to show others how to make potica, which can be intimidating to tackle on your own. She credits her mother for helping many people in the community gain the confidence to make it at home and have fun in the process. "She was so funny and such a good cook in everything that she made," says Debbie of her mother. "She loved to share and teach people to make the things she made that they liked. People loved to come to her class."

Her mom even got accolades from local priest Tom Radaich in a community cookbook where he reshared another of her signature recipes and wrote: "Sylvia Baraga was one of the greatest cooks I've known. I got to know her and her family at St. Joseph's in Chisolm when I was newly ordained, and 20 years later she came to my aid and cooked a couple of times a week at St. Leo's in Hibbing. I got the recipe for these wonderful big buns from her son David in St. Cloud. I am pretty sure that the material ingredients are right—I'm not sure how to add the essential ingredient of Sylvia's recipes and life—true self-sacrificing love and nurturing."

Today Debbie and her husband continue to draw from her mom's training when they make multiple batches of potica around the holidays to share with friends and family. It's a true labor of love and a process they have down pat, with Debbie making the dough and Greg tackling the filling with extreme attention to detail. The day before they are set to make potica, Greg goes through the walnuts one by one, ensuring they are in pristine shape, with no black parts that would cause bitterness in the filling. ➤➤

On their potica-making day, after the dough has risen and the filling is prepped, the real fun begins. Debbie spreads a sheet across her dining room table and lightly flours it. Then she and Greg carefully and quickly stretch the dough by hand across the width of the table until it is thin enough to read a newspaper underneath it.

"Making potica takes some patience and is time-intensive, but it's so thrilling when it comes out well," says Debbie, advising that it's best made with others to help with the delicate process of stretching the dough. Plus, it's more fun! After spreading the filling on top of the dough, the next step is to carefully and quickly roll it into one long log that's cut into three individual loaves for baking.

Aside from Christmas, Debbie's family occasionally makes potica at Easter. They've also made it for family weddings, including her son's nuptials, adding that it's common to see slices of potica at Iron Range celebrations as part of the dessert table. For holidays potica is typically served with morning coffee or alongside the main meal.

Debbie acknowledges the importance of her family's keepsake recipe and passing it on to the next generation. She and Greg have now taken on the role of teaching family members, including their grandchildren, who have been eager students and will carry on the tradition. "It's the memory of always having it at the holiday and the memories it evokes," says Debbie. "Everyone loves the taste of it, but it also brings back wonderful memories and smells of things you had at Christmastime."

Potica

MAKES 3 LOAVES

dough

1 cup milk

1 cup sugar

1 tablespoon salt

½ cup (1 stick) margarine

1 cup warm water

4 (¼-ounce) packets active dry yeast

4 eggs, beaten

8 cups flour

filling

3 pounds walnuts, ground

4½ cups sugar

½ teaspoon salt

½ cup honey

2 teaspoons vanilla

¾ cup (1½ sticks) butter

3 cups milk

3 eggs

Grease a large bowl for the dough and grease 3 (4x13–inch) loaf pans or a baking sheet; set aside.

In a large saucepan, heat 1 cup milk almost to boiling, then stir in 1 cup sugar, 1 tablespoon salt, and margarine; cool to lukewarm.

Measure warm water into a large bowl. Sprinkle yeast over water and stir until dissolved. Stir in lukewarm milk mixture, beaten eggs, and half of the flour (about 4 cups). Stir in remaining flour gradually to make a slightly stiff dough.

Turn dough onto lightly floured surface. Knead until smooth and elastic, about 8 minutes. Place dough in greased bowl, turning to grease top. Cover and let rise in a warm place for about 2 hours or until doubled in bulk.

Meanwhile, make filling by mixing ingredients in a large saucepan set over medium heat. Stir constantly until butter is melted and mixture comes to a boil. Set aside to cool.

When dough has risen, spread cloth or sheet on table and sprinkle lightly with flour. Place dough in the middle and stretch from the middle to the edges (see tip).

Spread filling over the stretched dough. Cut off thick edges. Roll like a jelly roll and cut into 3 loaves; place in prepared loaf pans or on baking sheet. Let rest for 30 minutes.

Bake at 300 degrees for 1 hour and 15 minutes.

tips It's important that your house is warm while you're stretching the dough, or you risk it drying out and becoming more susceptible to tears and holes. Debbie and Greg heat their house to 72 degrees on potica-making day.

While some may use a rolling pin to roll out and stretch the dough, Debbie's family does this process completely by hand. She advises starting from the center and, working quickly with a partner, gently stretching and pulling the dough—always keeping your hand flat, palm-side up.

Potica loaves can be baked on baking sheets, but Debbie prefers using three 4½x13x1½–inch loaf pans that belonged to her mother.

Potica stays well in the freezer and is easy to ship, making it great for gift giving.

For storage, Debbie recommends wrapping potica in aluminum foil.

There is more than one way to enjoy potica! It's delicious on its own, but Debbie likes to spread butter on a piece and enjoy it with coffee. Her sons like to eat it with a slice of ham and some horseradish.

just for fun The family has a cookbook of Sylvia's recipes that was given to all the brothers and sisters, nieces and nephews, so they can continue to make all of her favorite things and keep traditions alive.

It's no surprise that one of the biggest lessons Debbie learned from her mom, Sylvia, was the joy of cooking for loved ones. "My mom was so happy when she was in the kitchen. I remember it being a warm place where my mom would always be smiling, playing her favorite music (polka), cooking, and dancing."

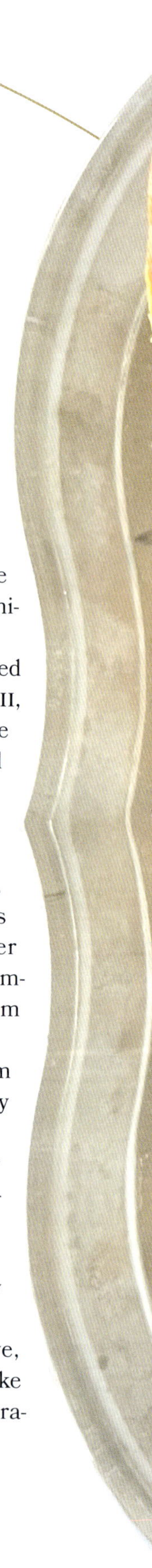

English Holiday Fruitcake

Kay Johnson
Cloquet, MN

the dish

A traditional holiday fruitcake with a modern twist: starting with a date bread mix.

the tell

For as long as Kay can remember, the holidays meant fruitcake and plum pudding, just as her English mother, Ida May "Bubbles" Bruley, had made them. Bubbles brought these cherished traditions with her when she immigrated to the United States aboard the *Queen Elizabeth I* in 1946.

Born and raised in North Thoresby, Grimsby, Lincolnshire, Bubbles served in the British Women's Auxiliary Air Force (WAAF) during World War II, caring for wounded soldiers in Wales and England. During this time she met and later married Clifford Bruley, a US Army truck driver stationed in England. Upon arriving in the United States they settled in Cloquet, Minnesota, with their young daughter, Shirley. Two more daughters, Kay and Jo, soon followed.

Bubbles was a devoted homemaker, known for her English charm, quick wit, warm hospitality, and love of baking. While she made pies year-round—favoring fresh strawberry-rhubarb in the summer—her Thanksgiving and Christmas desserts were legendary. No holiday was complete without her pumpkin and mincemeat pies, English Christmas plum pudding with white brandy sauce, and, of course, her fruitcakes.

Today her daughters carry on the holiday traditions they learned from their mom. Kay bakes the fruitcakes, Jo makes the plum pudding, and they send them to Shirley in Arizona, who happily contributes by eating them!

Kay also makes extra fruitcakes to share with friends or donate to her church's holiday bake sale. She laughs about fruitcake's reputation, encouraging skeptics to give it another try. While Bubbles once made her batter from scratch, she later switched to Pillsbury date bread mix, a shortcut Kay still swears by today.

The ingredients may have evolved, but the love, memories, and holiday spirit baked into each fruitcake remain unchanged—ensuring that Bubbles's holiday tradition lives on for generations to come.

MAKES 1 LARGE OR
2 SMALL LOAVES

1 egg

1 cup water

1 (16.6-ounce) box date quick bread mix (Pillsbury)

1 cup raisins

1 cup currants

1 cup candied red and green cherries, cut in half, plus more for decoration

1 cup mixed candied fruit

½ cup chopped nuts (walnuts or pecans), optional

¼ cup brandy, plus extra for brushing, optional

Heat oven to 350 degrees. Grease 1 (4x8–inch) loaf pan or 2 (2½x5–inch) loaf pans on bottom and sides; set aside.

In a large mixing bowl, whisk egg with 1 cup water. Stir in bread mix.

In separate bowl, combine raisins, currants, candied cherries, candied fruit, nuts (if using), and brandy (if using). Add fruit mixture to batter and mix well. Pour into prepared pan(s), placing 3 cherries on top for decoration.

Bake for approximately 1 hour, until an inserted toothpick or cake tester comes out clean. Smaller loaves may bake faster. Cool on waxed paper set on top of wire rack. Brush with brandy (if using). To freeze, wrap in waxed paper and place in plastic bag.

tip Kay says when she can't find the date bread mix in the grocery store, she orders it from Amazon.

Index

Abel, Mona Meittunen, 74–75
Akoori/Parsi Scrambled Eggs, 18–19
almonds: Crunchy Coleslaw, 126–27; Danish Puff, 27–29; Swedish Almond Rusks, 38–39
Anderson, Louella (and mother Dolly), 18–19
appetizers: BLT Bites, 116–17; Buffalo Chicken Dip, 112–13; Deviled Ham Cheese Ball, 179–80; Salami Chips, 115; Sue's Dip, 114
apples: Grandma Drake's Apple Butter, 55–57
Aunt Sally Cookies, 148–50
author's family: Becci (husband's cousin), 161; Carol (mom), vi, 1, 3, 5, 9, 32, 46, 62, 70, 72, 73, 76, 78–79, 83, 86, 91, 110, 115, 117, 130, 131–32, 142, 144, 156, 164, 166, 179, 189, 191, 196, 198, 212; Charlie (son), 212; Charlotte (husband's grandma), 7, 21, 33–34, 58; Ede (aunt), 1, 3, 6, 16, 62, 66, 86, 109; Eric Schmidt (cousin), 109; Frances (Grandma Meland), 3, 6, 14, 15, 166, 178, 187, 191; Gam (Myrtle, husband's grandma), 7, 178, 184, 212; Gerry (dad), vi, 32, 62, 70, 73, 91, 110, 198, 212; Hilma (Grandma Granley), 1, 3, 5–6, 9, 14, 33, 38–39, 82, 90; Jaye (husband), 6, 14, 108, 112, 118, 178, 184; Jeanette (husband's great-aunt), 149, 212; Jered (brother), 82–83; Linda (husband's cousin), 161, 163; Lucy (daughter), 63, 112, 142, 212; Mary Lou (mother-in-law), 3, 6, 21, 33–34, 58–59, 191

Baked French Toast, 22–23
Banana Bread, 50–51
bananas: Banana Bread, 50–51; Ede's (Kid-Friendly) Slush aka Tropical Banana Slush, 109
Becky's Birthday Cake, 137–39
beef: Ede's Meatballs, 66–67; Ham Balls, 68–69; Hamburger Soup, 91; Iron Range Pasties, 73–75; Juicy Lucy Tater Tot Hotdish, 63–65; Meatloaf Muffins, 73; Roast Beef and Pork with Gravy, 70–72
Betty's Caramels, 172–74
Biddle, Shansel (and Great-Grandmother Maria), 23, 212
BLT Bites, 116–17
Brandt, Becky, 90, 137, 139, 212
bread: Baked French Toast, 22–23; Cracked Wheat Bread, 101–3; Flatbread, 33–34; Grandma Rosamond's Family Bread, 104–5. *See also* pastries and sweet breads
Bromberg, Janet, 50–51
Buffalo Chicken Dip, 112–13

cakes: Becky's Birthday Cake, 137–39; Elaine's Pineapple Upside-Down Cake, 134–36; English Holiday Fruitcake, 210–11; Mom's One and Only Chocolate Cake, 131–33; Poppy Kuchen, 52–54; Rum Cake, 140–41; Self-Filled Cupcakes, 142–43; Sour Cream Somersault Cake, 44–45
candy: Betty's Caramels, 172–74
caramels: Betty's Caramels, 172–74
Carol's Christmas Jell-O, 196–97
Carol's Italian Shells, 78–79
carrots: Dill Butter Carrots, 84–85
Cheeley, Jeanie (and mother Rosamond), 104–5
Cheeley, Kara, 104
cheese: Buffalo Chicken Dip, 112–13; Cheesy Party Potatoes, 190–91; Chile Cheese Soup, 92–93; Deviled Ham Cheese Ball, 179–80; Sue's Dip, 114
cherries: Cherry Nut Bread, 46–47; Chocolate-Covered Cherry Bars, 198–99
chicken: Buffalo Chicken Dip, 112–13; Get Well Chicken Soup with Grandma Ev's Homemade Noodles, 94–97; Succulent Sesame Chicken, 76–77
Chile Cheese Soup, 92–93
chocolate: Chocolate Chip Shortbread Cookies, 144–45; Chocolate-Covered Cherry Bars, 198–99; Homemade Chocolate Pudding, 170–71; Jan's Club Cracker Bars, 154–55; Mom's One and Only Chocolate Cake, 131–33; Thunderstorm Bars, 158–60; Toffee Bars, 156–57
Chocolate Chip Shortbread Cookies, 144–45
Chocolate-Covered Cherry Bars, 198–99
Church Egg Dish, 16–17
coleslaw: Crunchy Coleslaw, 126–27
cookies and bars: Aunt Sally Cookies, 148–50; Chocolate Chip Shortbread Cookies, 144–45; Grandma Janet's White Cookies, 151–53; Jan's Club Cracker Bars, 154–55; Molasses Crinkle Cookies, 146–47; Mother's Sour Cream Cutout Cookies, 200–202; Rhubarb Pie Bars, 161–63; Swedish Almond Rusks, 38–39; Thunderstorm Bars, 158–60; Toffee Bars, 156–57
Cracked Wheat Bread, 101–3
Cranberry Fluff, 194–95
Creamy Cucumbers, 86–87
Crunchy Coleslaw, 126–27
cucumbers: Creamy Cucumbers, 86–87
cupcakes: Self-Filled Cupcakes, 142–43

Danish Puff, 27–29
Deviled Ham Cheese Ball, 179–80
Dill Butter Carrots, 84–85
Dill Pickle Pasta Salad, 124–25
dips and spreads: Buffalo Chicken Dip, 112–13; Grandma Drake's Apple Butter, 55–57; Rhubarb–Orange Slice Preserves, 58–59; Sue's Dip, 114
donuts: Grandma Olson's Buttermilk Donuts, 35–37
drinks: Ede's (Kid-Friendly) Slush aka Tropical Banana Slush, 109; Frothy Orange Juice, 15; Rhubarb Slush, 110–11
Dutch Pancake, 24–26

Easter Pie, 181–83
Ede's (Kid-Friendly) Slush aka Tropical Banana Slush, 109
Ede's Meatballs, 66–67
eggs: Akoori/Parsi Scrambled Eggs, 18–19; Baked French Toast, 22–23; Church Egg Dish, 16–17; Easter Pie, 181–83
Elaine's Pineapple Upside-Down Cake, 134–36
English Holiday Fruitcake, 210–11
Erickson-Mann, Patricia, 148–50

fish: Saltine Cracker Breaded Walleye, 82–83
Fitzgerald, Mary Kay (and Grandma McMahon), 192–93
Flamossa with Raspberry Sauce, 203–5
Flatbread, 33–34
Forstrom, Toni, 118, 212
Frothy Orange Juice, 15
Frozen Strawberry Dessert, 166–67
Get Well Chicken Soup with Grandma Ev's Homemade Noodles, 94–97
Grandma Drake's Apple Butter, 55–57
Grandma Helen's Cinnamon Coffee Cake Rolls, 40–43
Grandma Janet's White Cookies, 151–53
Grandma McMahon's Potato Dressing, 192–93
Grandma Olson's Buttermilk Donuts, 35–37
Grandma Rosamond's Family Bread, 104–5
gravy: Roast Beef and Pork with Gravy, 70–72

ham: Deviled Ham Cheese Ball, 179–80; Ham Balls, 68–69; Ham Loaf and Mustard Sauce, 184–86; Raisin Sauce (for Ham), 187
Ham Balls, 68–69
Hamburger Soup, 91
Ham Loaf and Mustard Sauce, 184–86
Hendrickson, Doreen, 110
Hlusak, Sarah, 48–49
Homemade Chocolate Pudding, 170–71
Homemade Noodles, 80–81
hotdishes/casseroles: Church Egg Dish, 16–17; Juicy Lucy Tater Tot Hotdish, 63–65

Iron Range Pasties, 73–75

Jackson, Kim, 98–100
Jan's Club Cracker Bars, 154–55
Johnson, Kay (and mother Ida May "Bubbles" Branley), 210–11, 212
Jones, Cathleen, 80–81
Juicy Lucy Tater Tot Hotdish, 63–65

Kimchi Jjigae, 98–100

Lamm Sisters (Carrie, Marcia, Liz), 158–60, 212
Layered Tortellini Salad, 122–23
Lux, Amelia, 148–50

Maguire, Jan, 154–55
Manske, Maria, 146, 212
meatballs: Ede's Meatballs, 66–67; Ham Balls, 68–69
Meatloaf Muffins, 73
Meittunen Family, 74–75
Mergenthal, Marie and Staci (and Grandma Janet), 124–25, 151–53, 212
Miggler, Sue, 114
molasses: Aunt Sally Cookies, 148–50; Molasses Crinkle Cookies, 146–47
Molasses Crinkle Cookies, 146–47
Mom's One and Only Chocolate Cake, 131–33
Morrow, Megan and John (and Grandma Cooper), 27, 29, 212
Mother's Sour Cream Cutout Cookies, 200–202
Murphy, Liz (and Grandma Betty), 173–74, 212

Nelson, Katie (and Grandma C and Grandma Margy), 53–54, 212
noodles: Get Well Chicken Soup with Grandma Ev's Homemade Noodles, 94–97; Homemade Noodles, 80–81. *See also* pasta

oranges: Frothy Orange Juice, 15; Rhubarb–Orange Slice Preserves, 58–59

pancakes: Dutch Pancake, 24–26; Sour Milk Griddle Cakes, 20–21
Passofaro, Jeannie, 181, 183
pasta: Carol's Italian Shells, 78–79; Dill Pickle Pasta Salad, 124–25; Get Well Chicken Soup with Grandma Ev's Homemade Noodles, 94–97; Homemade Noodles, 80–81; Layered Tortellini Salad, 122–23
pasties: Iron Range Pasties, 73–75
pastries and sweet breads: Banana Bread, 50–51; Cherry Nut Bread, 46–47; Danish Puff, 27–29; Grandma Helen's Cinnamon Coffee Cake Rolls, 40–43; Potica, 206–9; Pumpkin Bread with Blueberries, 48–49
Peanut Butter Pie, 168–69
Peterson, Julie, 126, 212
Peterson, Kara, 98, 126
Pletcher, Barb (and Grandmother Hansina), 203, 212
Poppy Kuchen, 52–54
pork: Roast Beef and Pork with Gravy, 70–72
potatoes: Cheesy Party Potatoes, 190–91; Grandma McMahon's Potato Dressing, 192–93
Potica, 206–9
Pumpkin Bread with Blueberries, 48–49

Raisin Sauce (for Ham), 187
raspberries: Flamossa with Raspberry Sauce, 203–5
Rhubarb Meringue Dessert, 164–65
Rhubarb–Orange Slice Preserves, 58–59
Rhubarb Pie Bars, 161–63
Rhubarb Slush, 110–11
Riepe, Jess (and Great-Grandmother Drake), 55, 57
Roast Beef and Pork with Gravy, 70–72
Rum Cake, 140–41

salads: Dill Pickle Pasta Salad, 124–25; Layered Tortellini Salad, 122–23
Salami Chips, 115
Saltine Cracker Breaded Walleye, 82–83
Sandwich Loaf, 118–21
Sarkinen, Chris and Christine, 112–13
sausage: Carol's Italian Shells, 78–79; Sausage Stuffing, 188–89
Sausage Stuffing, 188–89
Schumann Family (Kim, Jason, Joyce), 194–95, 212
Self-Filled Cupcakes, 142–43
Smith, Lori, 170
soups: Chile Cheese Soup, 92–93; Get Well Chicken Soup with Grandma Ev's Homemade Noodles, 94–97; Hamburger Soup, 91; Kimchi Jjigae, 98–100
Sour Cream Somersault Cake, 44–45
Sour Milk Griddle Cakes, 20–21
strawberries: Frozen Strawberry Dessert, 166–67
Succulent Sesame Chicken, 76–77
Sue's Dip, 114
Swedish Almond Rusks, 38–39

Theis-Mahon, Nikki (and Grandmother Elaine), 134–36, 212
Thomas, Jeanie, 90, 92, 101
Thomas, Linda, 92, 101–3
Thomasser, Shannon (and Grandma Helen), 40–43, 90
Thunderstorm Bars, 158–60
Toffee Bars, 156–57
tomatoes: BLT Bites, 116–17; Carol's Italian Shells, 78–79; Hamburger Soup, 91
True, Sharon, 169

Vandenberg, Jami (and Grandma Olson), 35, 37, 90
Vidmar, Debbie and Greg (and mother Sylvia), 207–9, 212

walleye: Saltine Cracker Breaded Walleye, 82–83
Walter, Catherine, 200, 202
water bath canning method, 58
Wilkie, Carol (and Grandma Ev), 94, 97

Zeto, Julie, 24, 26

Fruit Salad
Lemon pudding
fruit cocktail
1 pineapple chunks
2 c marshmallows
4 bananas
any other fruit

Photo captions

3 left: Mom and me; right: me with my mother-in-law, Mary Lou

19 Dolly holding Lea; Louella and Mario in front, ca. 1961

22 left: Great-Grandmother Maria with a friend; right: This photo, from 1925, was taken outside the school Maria's eight children, including Shansel's grandpa Edgar (top left), attended.

29 Grandma Cooper

39 Grandma Hilma with me (left), my cousin Anne, and my brother Chris

52 Grandma Margy and grandkid Ambrose

61 top right: I found this recipe for ham balls (see page 69), in Toni's writing, tucked in my mom's recipe box on the back of a thank-you card Toni wrote to my parents after her wedding.

65 Lucy and me, dropping off our entries at the Minnesota State Fair

66 Aunt Ede

83 top: My brothers Jered and Chris with fish; bottom: My dad with his prized catch. He loved fishing even though an allergy prevented him from eating fish.

88 top left: Carol Wilkie's recipe box was hand-painted by her mom (see page 94); bottom left: Carol's fun packaging for her homemade soup.

99 Kim Jackson with her parents, Marlys and Howard

106 Nikki Theis-Mahon's vintage cake carrier

107 top right: Julie Peterson's grandma's spice cabinet and a cutting board with her mom's chili recipe engraved on it (see page 126)

132 My kids Lucy and Charlie request this cake every year for their birthdays.

134 Elaine and her husband, Herman

139 top: Becky, age nine; bottom: Becky with her mom, Karen

146 Maria and her mom, Helen

148 top left: Jeanette on her birthday; bottom left: the family cookbook (see page 150)

152 bottom middle: Grandma Janet had a special sugar shaker that Staci is lucky to have today; bottom left: Staci and Grandma Janet on their day of baking

159 Carrie and friend Catherine with the bars

174 Liz with a photo of Betty

176 top left: My mom, Carol, with her famous Christmas Jell-O (see page 196)

185 Gam and a few of the many holiday menus she left behind

195 top right: Grandma Goodyear; middle right: *The Fron Centennial Cookbook* was compiled by the Fron Lutheran Church (ELCA) Women in Starbuck, Minnesota, in 1980 to mark the church's centennial. The cover has a Norwegian title, "vær så god," which means "here you are, there you are" (said when handing something over to someone) as well as "you're welcome."

203 Grandma Hansina and Great-Aunt Stina

208 top: Debbie's mom, Sylvia; middle: Debbie and grandsons stretching the dough; bottom: Debbie's nieces Karly and Tamy making potica

210 Bubbles in the Women's Auxiliary Air Force (WAAF)

Weights & Measures

weights / measures / equivalents

Dash = less than ⅛ teaspoon

3 teaspoons = 1 tablespoon

16 tablespoons = 1 cup

1 cup = ½ pint

2 cups = 1 pint (16 ounces)

2 pints = 4 cups = 1 quart

4 quarts = 1 gallon

8 quarts = 1 peck

4 pecks = 1 bushel

to measure cups by tablespoons

⅛ cup = 2 tablespoons

¼ cup = 4 tablespoons

⅓ cup = 5⅓ tablespoons

½ cup = 8 tablespoons

⅔ cup = 10⅔ tablespoons

¾ cup = 12 tablespoons

1 cup = 16 tablespoons

butter

1 stick = ½ cup

2 sticks = 1 cup

1 pound = 2 cups

Acknowledgments

Thanks to all the "cooks in the kitchen" who helped turn my vision into reality.

I am beyond grateful to each and every recipe contributor who graciously shared their time to dish and tell with me, welcoming me into their kitchens and giving me a seat at their table. Your family stories and heartfelt recipes have been such an inspiration to me and a reminder of why I set out on this path in the first place.

Thank you to the Minnesota Historical Society Press for giving me the opportunity to create a book that is deeply personal and from the heart. Special thanks to Shannon Pennefeather, a true angel of an editor who radiates positivity and gave me the time and space I needed while helping shape every page with care.

Thanks to designer Susan Everson for bringing these stories and recipes to life and designing a cookbook I am so very proud of! Heartfelt thanks to Minnesota mavens Stephanie Hansen and Patrice Johnson, whose inspiring cookbooks and generous words of wisdom encouraged me as I began this journey.

To Rachael White from Set the Table Photography, thank you for coming in at the eleventh hour with your talented food styling eye and exceptional photography skills and for making the process so much fun. And to Allie Mellman—thank you for helping me from the very beginning to create a blog and space where I could find my voice.

Thank you to my mom, Carol, and my mother-in-law, Mary Lou—the essential conduits to our family recipes and food traditions. I appreciate you more than you know. From all the hours you've logged in the kitchen, whether preparing daily meals or elaborate holiday feasts, you both make it look so easy!

To Jaye—thank you for never complaining about the piles of dirty dishes, the endless grocery lists, or the fact that I spent so much time cooking and baking things you didn't always get to eat. Thank you to Lucy and Charlie for your support and encouragement. I hope this book becomes a keepsake that you'll turn to whenever you need a taste of home.

And to my dear dad—my guiding star—thank you for giving me the nudge to write this book and for believing in me, even when I didn't. You didn't get to see it finished, but I felt you with me every step of the way. This book is for you, with all my heart. I hope it makes you proud.

Sarah Peterson is a passionate home cook and storyteller who draws inspiration from tried-and-true family recipes handed down through multiple generations. When she is not in the kitchen of her 120-year-old house, she can be found scouring estate sales and vintage shops to feed her obsession for old recipe boxes, church cookbooks, and pretty dishes. A lifelong (and very proud) Minnesotan who loves snow and winter, Sarah dreams of living the "lake life" and can never get enough of the Minnesota State Fair. She lives in St. Paul with her husband, Jaye, and dog, Dolly, and is constantly planning what to cook when her adult kids, Lucy and Charlie, come home for a visit.